PENGUIN CLASSICS

THE SECRET HISTORY

ADVISORY EDITOR: BETTY RADICE

Procopius was born at Caesarea, the great city built by Herod on the coast of Palestine. We do not know the date: it was probably A.D. 500 or a little before. After practising at Byzantium as an advocate and rhetorician he became in A.D. 527 private secretary and legal adviser to Belisarius, whom he accompanied on his first three campaigns, in Persia, Africa, and Italy, and by whom he was entrusted with important missions. When Belisarius, after capturing Ravenna, was recalled to Byzantium, Procopius went with him, and it is probable that when in the next year Belisarius was again sent to the eastern front his secretary once more accompanied him. But twelve months later, in A.D. 542, he was certainly back in the capital, where he witnessed the terrible plague which visited that city, and which he was able to describe in graphic detail. We do not know whether he was with the general during the years of his second campaign in and around Italy, which he describes less minutely, or what he did with his time, apart from literary work, during the remaining years of his life. He must have been in the Emperor's good books, as in A.D. 560 he was given the exalted rank of *illustris*; and it is probable that he was the Procopius who two years later was Prefect of the City. The date of his death is not known with absolute certainty; but he seems to have outlived Justinian, and some scholars state positively that he died very late in A.D. 565. If so, we have the strange coincidence that Belisarius, Justinian, and Procopius all died in the same year. But such a coincidence is by no means unique in history.

From Procopius's pen three works have come down to us, commonly known as *The Histories*, *Buildings*, and *The Secret History*.

G. A. Williamson was born in 1895 and was a Classical Exhibitioner at Worcester College, Oxford, graduating with a First Class Honours degree. He was Senior Classics Master at Norwich School from 1922 to 1960. He has also translated *Josephus: The Jewish War* (1959) and *Eusebius: The History of the Church* (1965) for the Penguin Classics. G. A. Williamson died in 1982.

PROCOPIUS

THE SECRET HISTORY

TRANSLATED
WITH AN INTRODUCTION BY
G. A. WILLIAMSON

PENGUIN BOOKS

PENGUIN BOOKS

Published by the Penguin Group
Penguin Books Ltd, 80 Strand, London WC2R 0RL, England
Penguin Putnam Inc., 375 Hudson Street, New York, New York 10014, USA
Penguin Books Australia Ltd, 250 Camberwell Road, Camberwell, Victoria 3124, Australia
Penguin Books Canada Ltd, 10 Alcorn Avenue, Toronto, Ontario, Canada M4V 3B2
Penguin Books India (P) Ltd, 11 Community Centre, Panchsheel Park, New Delhi – 110 017, India
Penguin Books (NZ) Ltd, Cnr Rosedale and Airborne Roads, Albany, Auckland, New Zealand
Penguin Books (South Africa) (Pty) Ltd, 24 Sturdee Avenue, Rosebank 2196, South Africa

Penguin Books Ltd, Registered Offices: 80 Strand, London WC2R 0RL, England

www.penguin.com

This translation first published 1966
Reprinted with Select Bibliography 1981
21

Copyright © G. A. Williamson, 1966
All rights reserved

Set in Monotype Bembo
Printed in England by Clays Ltd, St Ives plc

Contents

Introduction

The Secret History is a remarkable work, informative and interesting, vivid and original, but presenting us with most unusual problems. The title by which it is usually known suits it well enough, but is of late Latin origin and bears no resemblance to the Greek title, for which likewise the author was not responsible. The Greeks called it the *Anecdota*, which Gibbon misleadingly translated 'Anecdotes'. The word *Anecdota*, which was applied to it by the lexicographer Suidas, means 'Unpublished things', and was used because the book was not published in the author's lifetime. We cannot say how long after his death it was published – if indeed it was, in the ordinary sense, published at all. Here then is our first problem: why was the book written, if it could not be published?

The second problem is how the author came to write a book which seems to fly in the face of all that he had written before, and to be still more difficult to reconcile with what he wrote later. Did he twice change his mind? Did he at each stage believe what he was writing? Was he writing for different groups of readers? Was he really the author of all the books, or has his name been mistakenly attached to the middle one, which seems to sort so ill with the others? This too is a problem which we are not yet in a position to tackle.

Leaving both problems aside for the present let us take a general look at our author and his book. Procopius lived at an eventful time, a time that stands out in history because

7

it saw the death of the Classical Period and the birth of the Middle Ages. In the days of his father the western half of the Roman Empire had collapsed, and on the seven hills beside the Tiber there was no longer an imperial city, able *regere imperio populos*. The city of Constantine was now the sole capital, mistress of a community that still called itself Roman but from which Roman politics, Roman morals and religion, Roman architecture, and even Roman dress had disappeared. The time at which Procopius lives stands out all the more because he wrote about it, and wrote about it so revealingly. There was so much to record about that time that he was able to write volume after volume about it, writing from first-hand knowledge and personal experience, and rarely attempting to record events of an earlier day.

There are those who explain the course of history by reference to economic and other material causes. For Procopius history was made by persons, sometimes by God Himself but generally by human beings, swayed by human passions though perhaps subject to demonic influences; indeed, they might actually be themselves demons in human form. His books are not biographies but histories, in which events both on the battlefield and in cities, palaces, and homes are set down in the greatest detail; but they are primarily books about persons. This is true of *The Secret History* even more than of the other works. Here we read of little else than the doings, motives, and characters of two men and two women; and the many others who make brief appearances in the pages of this little book are introduced solely because of what they did on behalf of these four or suffered at their hands. The two men were Justinian, sometimes called the Great, for forty-seven years ruler of the

8

Roman Empire, and Belisarius, the outstanding soldier of his day and one of the greatest generals who ever commanded the armies of the Romans. The two women, so important because of their dominating characters and total lack of principle, were Theodora, for twenty-five years the consort of Justinian and joint ruler of the Empire, and Antonina, the irresistible enchantress whose husband Belisarius was powerless in her hands. How important in the story are these four may be judged from the fact that out of every twenty pages of this book Antonina appears on three, Belisarius on four, Theodora on ten, and Justinian on eighteen.

The period with which we are chiefly concerned extends from the birth of Procopius to the writing of *The Secret History*, a period of fifty years forming the first half of the sixth century of our era. It was a period filled with wars and riots, plagues, earthquakes, and floods, filled also with enormous creative activity in architecture and the arts. Before examining the course of events during those fifty years, let us place them in their setting by sketching in barest outline the historical phases that led up to them.

From the day in 27 B.C. when he assumed the title of Augustus till the day of his death forty years later Octavianus Caesar, the first of the Imperial line, was careful to call himself *princeps*, the first citizen, and eschewing pomp to preserve the illusion that power remained in the hands of senate and people and of the historic magistracies. His example was largely followed by his successors for some three centuries, though with the increase of centralization and bureaucracy the pretence wore very thin. But with Diocletian, who ascended the throne in A.D. 284, it was dropped altogether. Power was divided between two Augusti and two Caesars, Diocletian occupying the first place. That power knew no constitutional limits. The rulers were openly recognized for the unbridled autocrats they were. Simplicity gave way to pomp and majesty, western dignity to oriental splendour. The *princeps* became the *dominus*, lord and master, and his fellow-citizens his subjects and bondservants. The linen toga was replaced by elaborately adorned garments of silk, the headband or wreath by a jewelled crown. Before His Majesty even the noblest must make humble obeisance. The four rulers established their own capitals in Gaul, Italy, the Balkans, and Asia Minor. Rome no longer counted.

When Diocletian abdicated, a fight to the death broke out between the remaining three, and there were no fewer than six rivals for domination by the time that the young Constantine began the struggle that was to end in his becoming sole ruler of the whole Empire. His reign was noteworthy for two events of immense importance – the recognition of Christianity as not merely a permitted religion but the religion of the State, and the establishment of a new capital at the old Greek colony of Byzantium, henceforth generally spoken of as Constantinople, but always referred to by Procopius under its old name. Rome, as already noted, belonged to the past.

The peace which this great emperor brought was as short-lived as himself, and on his death the old rivalries were resumed, his three surviving sons battling with each other. So it came about that only twenty-seven years later the Empire was again divided, Valens taking the East and Valentinian the West. Divided it remained except for the brilliant but brief reign of Theodosius, which was followed by a series of 'barbarian' incursions into Italy so overwhelming that in 476 the Empire of the West finally collapsed, and the last emperor, whose name through the irony of history was Romulus Augustulus, abdicated. From then on there was only the Empire centred in Byzantium, but it was to endure nearly a thousand years longer, till Byzantium itself was stormed by the Turks, Constantine XIII killed fighting to the last, and the Crescent set up in the Church of the Holy Wisdom, one of the greatest marvels of Christian art, and an enduring monument to the emperor who is the leading figure in *The Secret History*.

When poor Romulus laid down his authority, the throne of the East had for two years been occupied by Zeno, the first of the four emperors who figure in Procopius's pages. Zeno receives only a passing mention. Anastasius, who succeeded him in A.D. 491, is introduced more than once because he provides a contrast with Justinian: the former filled the Treasury, the latter emptied it; the former made ample provision for the soldiers on active service, the latter starved and robbed them. Of Justin there was more to be said, because as uncle to Justinian he made it possible for Justinian to succeed him: he allowed his nephew to be virtual ruler of the Empire throughout his own nominal reign, and made him officially joint emperor some months before his death. Moreover, by tampering with the law he enabled the foolish young man to wed the unspeakable Theodora, and so to bring miseries untold upon the Roman people. Having thus disposed in a few pages of three emperors, whose combined reigns totalled forty-four years, our author devotes the rest of his book to the reign of

Justinian, or rather to the first twenty-three years of that reign, which he regarded as wholly calamitous.

Of peasant stock, the child of Gothic parents, Flavius Anicianus Justinianus was born at Tauresium (Skoplje) in Illyricum, probably in A.D. 483. Adopted as son by his uncle Justinus or Justin, he made himself so popular with both senate and people that he was elected consul and given the rank of *Nobilissimus*. Justin, a mercenary adventurer, had rendered such services to Anastasius that in 418 he became successor to that monarch. He was already an old man – as Procopius says, with one foot in the grave – far too old to carry out efficiently the duties of his exalted position; he was, moreover, as stupid as a donkey, and so illiterate that he was unable even to sign his own name. He lasted only nine years, and in A.D. 527 was succeeded by his adopted son, who with his wife as joint monarch now wielded alone the powers which before that he had shared with Justin. The Empress was to reign for twenty-one years, her husband for thirty-eight, if we count from Justin's death.

Justinian had married Theodora four years before their accession, having persuaded his uncle to abolish the long-established law forbidding a senator to marry a harlot, which all the world knew that Theodora was. Justinian was thirty-nine or forty, Theodora only twenty, perhaps not even that: she had not been born till some date in the first decade of the century. She had, however, packed a great deal into those few years. She had been born in Byzantium, or, as some said, in Cyprus, the home of Aphrodite. Her father was a bear-feeder in the Amphitheatre. At a very early age she went on the stage as a knock-about comedienne, and at the first possible moment became, like her two sisters, a prostitute of the lowest type, giving herself up to three different vices, one of them unnameable even in our own outspoken days. Her vulgarity was appalling, and her lust, if Procopius is to be believed, unparalleled and insatiable. We need not anticipate here his detailed and revolting description. She conceived repeatedly, and except on one unfortunate occasion succeeded in murdering her unborn children. Then she met Justinian, who became her helpless slave, made her his mistress, and as soon as permission was given took her to wife.

Theodora was much more than a wife to the Emperor, albeit a faithful wife, to judge from the fact that from the time of their marriage no more imputations were made against the propriety of her personal behaviour, apart from her alleged passion for her servant Areobindus – a scandal which she disposed of by having him savagely flogged and making sure that he was never seen again. She was also Justinian's adviser in every sphere of government, and provided the stability which he lacked. Procopius more than once insists that he was as changeable as a weathercock, while she was determined and relentless. He owed a great deal to her, especially in the terrible days of the Nika insurrection, when he lost his head completely, panicked, and was ready to flee, but she stood her ground undaunted, saving the situation for them both, and making him yet more her slave. She was helped, of course, by the fact that she was not merely his consort but joint ruler with him, so that she could receive the ambassadors of foreign monarchs, insist that the Emperor's officials should swear an oath of allegiance to her as to him, and compel her visitors to grovel on the ground before her, a thing which her predecessors had never done.

It is small wonder that she was universally feared, especially as she appears to have been bloodthirsty, merciless, and sadistic. Procopius has much to say on this subject, and says it with vigour and emphasis; and his evidence on this point, as in the matter of her conduct before marriage, is corroborated by a number of Greek and Latin writers of quite early date, one of whom tells us, for instance, that she swore by the Almighty to flay a certain messenger alive – *per Viventem in saecula excoriari te faciam*. At the same time she was credited with great generosity towards the poor: but it is easy to be generous if one has enough left to satisfy every whim, and no scruples at all about piling up vast wealth at the expense of other people. Opinions will differ about her most original plan to clean up the forum of Byzantium by roping in all the five hundred prostitutes who plied their trade there, and locking them up in a sort of reformatory on the other side of the strait – a fate to which, according to Procopius, many of them preferred suicide.

Whatever she was like as a wife, Theodora made a very unsatisfactory parent. As we have seen, she regularly practised abortion. On one occasion she failed to take the necessary measures in time, and bore a son to one of her lovers, who acknowledged the child as his, and knowing only too well the ferocity and unscrupulousness of the youthful mother carried him off to the safety of Arabia. After the father's death the boy ventured to return to Byzantium; his mother took one look at him, and he was never seen again. She also gave birth to a daughter, presumably when she was mistress or wife of Justinian. Of this daughter we only know that she presented her mother with a grandson, whose life the heartless woman ruined by forcing him to become engaged to the daughter of Belisarius, and to live with the immature girl against the wishes of them both, by this means engineering a lucrative marriage which the girl's parents had striven to prevent.

Thus Theodora extended to her own offspring the cruelty which she had practised throughout her reign against one person or another, and against every class of her subjects. The boy Anastasius must have been almost the last of her victims, for a few months after the forced marriage she was dead. She was still in her forties: her husband was to live twice as long. The cause of her death was cancer, and there is evidence that she had felt it coming. Of this woman Bryce wrote, 'About the beauty, the intellectual gifts, and the imperious will of Theodora there can be no doubt. She was evidently an extraordinary person, born to shine in any station of life.' As such she has fascinated writers, especially between the years 1879 and 1885, which saw the appearance of Pottinger's romance *Blue and Green*, of Débidour's enthusiastic study *The Empress Theodora*, and of plays by Rhangabé and Sardou, both entitled *Theodora*. Perhaps the French can appreciate the lady better than we can.

We return now to the widower, at this stage a man of sixty-five. He never married again. Perhaps there was no one fit to take Theodora's place; or perhaps he had had enough of married life and enjoyed being his own master once more. Procopius tells us little of the later years of his reign; for *The Secret History* was written only two years after Theodora's death. The *Histories* were completed four years later, and the remaining work, published five years before the Emperor's death, was concerned mainly with his work as a builder.

Since the present work consists mainly of a detailed account of Justinian's doings, there is no need for us to do more than consider his reign in the broadest outline. We may accept as our starting-point the summing up of J. B. Bury: 'Justinian was a great conqueror, a great lawgiver, a great diplomat, and a great builder. He was also the protector and leader of the church.'

The greatest of these achievements was in the realm of law. Justinian had not long occupied the throne before he commissioned ten experts to clear away the existing confusion by drawing up a *Corpus Iuris Civilis*. Two years after his accession he promulgated *Codex Constructionum*, followed four years later by the famous Digest, which comprised no fewer than fifty volumes. It is upon these consolidations of the law that the legal systems of many countries are built to this day. Whether Justinian was really devoted to the rule of law may however be doubted. The only allusions to the subject in our book are denunciations of his readiness to change the law in his own interest or to suit the whim of his partner, and to cancel existing statutes if adequately bribed by one party to a lawsuit and then re-enact them on receipt of a bigger bribe from his opponent.

The protection and leading of the church took the form of attempting to compel pagans to accept the State religion – in Asia Minor alone seventy thousand were forcibly baptized – and to compel all who were nominally Christian to accept the decisions of the Council of Chalcedon. This involved wholesale and merciless persecution, which served chiefly to alienate his subjects, especially in Egypt, and open the way for the irruption of Mohammedanism a century later. It may be stated without hesitation that his efforts did nothing but injury to the cause of Christ.

His architectural projects were on a vast scale: the number, size, and beauty of the buildings for which he was responsible were alike immense. It is not his fault that so few have survived to our own time. But they were erected at enormous cost, and at such a time this vast expenditure on buildings, nominally raised to the glory of God but calculated to enhance that of their originator, could hardly be justified. The situation of the Empire was precarious in the extreme. All round its frontiers the warlike tribes were poised to strike; indeed in Justinian's own reign they reached the walls of the capital and terrified its citizens. To spend money, public money, thus was very like fiddling while Rome burned. Procopius takes Justinian to task on two particular counts – that for the express purpose of killing off the inhabitants of Byzantium he refused to repair the aqueduct on which their water-supply depended, and that he spent great sums on erecting along the beaches structures which were intended to keep back the waters of the Bosporus. The writer has been critized on the ground that the Emperor was endeavouring to provide his subjects with defences against the encroachment of these waters; but was it not rather to protect the mansions which he, like his wealthy predecessors in Republican times, loved to build for himself at the water's edge?

On the defence of the Empire Justinian did of course spend money freely. Much of it went to bribe his dangerous neighbours to forgo their incursions into his territory, a form of diplomacy which in the long run was bound to be ruinous. He made further inroads into the funds bequeathed to him by his prudent predecessor, the Emperor Anastasius, in order to maintain large armies in the field. These were not formed of citizen levies as in the brave days of old; the manhood of the capital were not prepared to leave their comfort, their money-making, and their pleasures to face the dangers and privations of a distant campaign as their fathers had done. They left the defence of their fatherland to mercenaries, and their fighting instincts found expression only in murderous and senseless partisan strife between the rival Blue and Green factions. Justinian's armies consisted of a motley collection of contingents contributed by a variety of half-civilized races, moulded into a magnificent fighting force by the genius of one man, a man to whom the Emperor owed nearly all the victories won during his reign, and whom he treated with meanness, ingratitude, and distrust. It was not he but Belisarius who was the great conqueror. What the situation called for was the establishment of defensible frontiers, even if that meant his withdrawing from some of the territory governed by his predecessors, just as the wise Hadrian had abandoned most of the ground conquered by his less prudent predecessor Trajan. But Justinian, like so many rulers before and after him, was bent on extending his dominions, and used his armies and their brilliant commander to recover the western provinces of Africa, Sicily, and Italy. Belisarius was successful; but Italy had to be fought over a second time, and could not long be held.

Justinian was hardly in his grave before his house of cards began to collapse. In A.D. 568 the northern half of Italy was conquered by the Lombards. Then Pannonia and Dacia fell to the Avars, who had come all the way from the Caspian, and proceeded to found a Slav–Bulgar empire. They swept southwards into the Balkans and exacted tribute from Justinian's successors. A generation after his death the eastern provinces were overrun by the Persians. There was no one to do for the Emperor Maurice what Belisarius had done for Justinian.

Thus it may safely be said that apart from the consolidation of Roman law Justinian accomplished little of permanent value, and that Procopius's unfavourable comparison of him with Anastasius is hardly surprising.

It is time now to say something of Belisarius and Antonina. Like his master, Belisarius came from Illyricum, but he was a much younger man, born probably in A.D. 505. After service in the Emperor's bodyguard he became at twenty-five – an age similar to that of Hannibal and Napoleon – Commander in the East, where at Daras in Mesopotamia, though seriously outnumbered, he defeated the Persians. A year later, however, he was himself defeated at Callinicum on the Euphrates. He was recalled, but without dishonour. Never again was he to suffer defeat. The next year, A.D. 532, he was faced with a very different task. The great Nika revolt took place, in which the Blues and the Greens combined to place Justinian in the utmost danger, and blood ran freely. The young officer, showing tact, resourcefulness, and immense courage, stepped into the breach and quelled the furious mob in the Hippodrome, a service which a better man than Justinian would never have forgotten.

Having recovered his confidence Justinian, blind to the pressing danger from east and north, resolved to recover the lost provinces in the west, and in the following years sent

Belisarius at the head of an army only fifteen thousand strong – a fifth of the number that little Rome, after three defeats at Hannibal's hands, had sent nearly seven and a half centuries before to face him at Cannae – to dispose of Gelimer and his Vandal host in Africa. Julius Caesar had found infantry always more than a match for any cavalry available in his day. But Belisarius realized that heavy men, heavily armed and mounted on heavy horses, could be used to devastating effect, as Robert Graves explains with great thoroughness in his historical novel *Count Belisarius*. Belisarius certainly did use them to devastating effect, and after twice defeating the Vandals and capturing their king he was able to return after a single campaign, enriched with vast loot, enough to supply his own needs for many a day. He also brought back with him the Seven-branched Golden Lampstand which Titus had removed from the Sanctuary of Herod's Temple in Jerusalem on the day when that wonderful edifice went up in flames; his father Vespasian had placed it in his great Temple of Peace in Rome; and only fifty years before the birth of Belisarius a Vandal king had conveyed it to Carthage. The victorious 'Roman' presented it to Justinian, who sent it back to its original home, Jerusalem. Justinian rewarded his overwhelming success by allowing him to celebrate a 'triumph' through the streets of Byzantium, and by striking a medal in his honour.

The next year he was sent to yet a third area of conflict. He began by recovering Sicily; then he crossed to Italy and captured first Naples, then Rome, where he was besieged for a year by the Ostrogoths but emerged victorious. Four years after that he captured Ravenna and took prisoner the Gothic king, Vittigis. It was a splendid achievement, and the Goths held him in such respect that they offered to set him on the imperial throne. Being then as throughout his life devotedly loyal to his emperor, he defied all precedent by refusing. Justinian nevertheless summoned him to the capital and received him coldly, alleging the danger that threatened once more on the Persian front. The danger was very real. King Chosroes was a formidable enemy, ready at all times to pour his troops into Roman territory. The Emperor had no option but to employ once more the faithful servant of whom he was so jealous, and Belisarius spent the next three years campaigning for the second time against Rome's enemies in the east. But his removal from Italy had left a vacuum which the Goths had not been slow to fill, and the indispensable general was switched thousands of miles from the eastern frontier to the western. His forces were, however, quite inadequate, and no provision was made by Justinian even for the payment of the troops. Five years' effort produced but little result, and the unfortunate commander was recalled, being replaced by the eunuch Narses.

How much Belisarius might have accomplished for Justinian, had that ungrateful and short-sighted monarch provided him with a fraction of the backing that he needed and deserved! The military genius, now comparable in age with Cromwell and Marlborough, was forced to spend ten years in retirement, until in A.D. 559 the Huns swarmed round the wall of Byzantium itself, and in this desperate emergency he was called on to improvise measures to save the threatened city. Once more his courage and resourcefulness prevailed, and the danger was averted. Even this did not mitigate the resentment and suspicion which his every act aroused in the Emperor, and three years later an absurd charge of conspiracy was brought against him, and he was imprisoned and deprived of all his property. We need not accept the picturesque but much later story that he was blinded and died a beggar. We know that he was restored to favour, though never again employed, and that he died on the thirteenth of March A.D. 565, anticipating the death of his master by exactly eight months. From first to last he had shown himself a man of devoted loyalty and astonishing ability, and of high principles that show a marked contrast with the selfishness and depravity that surrounded him. The only faults with which we are in a position to charge him are those set forth so mercilessly in the denigrating pages of *The Secret History*.

Chief of these faults was the weakness of character that put him at the mercy of the enticement, wiles, and if Procopius is to be believed, the spells or love-potions of the sorceress, his wife. Antonina was fully qualified to become the friend, ally, and partner in abominations of the Empress Theodora. Her father and grandfather had been charioteers and the associates of magicians, her mother a street-walker. She spent her own early years in the same way, and again and again became a mother. She seems to have married twice. Her first husband she presented with a son, Photius, her second (Belisarius) with a daughter Joannina. She was many years older than Belisarius, and perhaps he realized that she would never bear him a son; for before his expedition to Libya he adopted a youth called Theodosius. Marriage had not improved his wife's morals nor satisfied the demands of her body, and it was not long before she conceived an uncontrollable passion for her adopted son, with whom she

22

had intercourse even before the eyes of servants. Such was her power over her husband that even when he caught them in the act she silenced him with her brazen denials of guilt. At last a woman slave, with two boys who had the care of the bedchamber, under a sworn guarantee of secrecy reported to the poor cuckold all that was going on. But the enchantress convinced him that his informants were lying, drove him into betraying them to her, cut out their tongues, and carved them up. She then persuaded him to kill Constantine, a general who as Belisarius's friend had dared to express sympathy for him.

Nothing could keep the elderly adulteress and her youthful lover apart. For a time he lay low in Ephesus and professed to be a monk. But he was soon back, driving his indignant foster-father and Antonina's son Photius to make an agreement that Photius should run the miscreant to earth. The latter fled once more to Ephesus and took sanctuary in the cathedral, but was sold to Photius by the archbishop himself. Photius sent him under guard into Cilicia; but the Empress, with whom Antonina was hand in glove, rewarded her for services rendered in the destruction of Pope Silverius and others by fetching him back to Byzantium, where she hid him for a time and then presented him to her friend as a pearl, the most beautiful that had ever been seen. Evidently Theodora, who is supposed to have left all her sins behind her when she married Justinian and to have become a model wife, had no scruples about aiding and abetting the infamous conduct of another man's wife, and wrecking the life of her own husband's most faithful servant. Nor had her friend any scruples about accepting Theodora's help in getting rid of her unwanted son Photius. With her approval the Empress tortured him and cast him into prison, whence at the third attempt he escaped, to spend the rest of his life in Jerusalem under the protection of a monk's cowl.

Such then were the four persons in comparison with whom all others mentioned in this book are of little account. Can we trust the book and accept it as factual? Before attempting to answer that question let us summarize what is known of its author, of whom it may be said at once that as a contemporary of almost all the people of whom he writes, as a prominent citizen of Byzantium acquainted with many of the leading men of his days, as the companion of Belisarius and Antonina – for Antonina accompanied her husband on all his earlier expeditions – and as an educated, intelligent, and observant man and a capable writer, he was well qualified to compose the works that he bequeathed to the world.

Procopius was born at Caesarea, the great city built by Herod on the coast of Palestine. We do not know the date: it was probably A.D. 500 or a little before. After practising at Byzantium as an advocate and rhetorician he became in A.D. 527 private secretary and legal adviser to Belisarius, whom he accompanied on his first three campaigns, in Persia, Africa, and Italy, and by whom he was entrusted with important missions. When Belisarius after capturing Ravenna was recalled to Byzantium, Procopius went with him, and it is probable that when in the next year Belisarius was again sent to the eastern front his secretary once more accompanied him. But twelve months later, in A.D. 542, he was certainly back in the capital, where he witnessed the terrible plague which visited that city, and which he was able to describe in graphic detail. We do not know whether he was with the general during the years of his second campaign in and around Italy, which he describes less minutely, or what he did with his time, apart from literary work, during the remaining years of his life. He must have been in the Emperor's good books, as in A.D. 560 he was given the exalted rank of *illustris*; and it is probable that he was the Procopius who two years later was Prefect of the City. The date of his death is not known with absolute certainty; but he seems to have outlived Justinian, and some scholars state positively that he died very late in A.D. 565. If so, we have the strange coincidence that Belisarius, Justinian, and Procopius all died in the same year. But such a coincidence is by no means unique in history.

From Procopius's pen three works have come down to us, commonly known as *The Histories*, *Buildings*, and *The Secret History*. The first and longest work was entitled by its author *The Discourses about the Wars*. It consists of eight books: two of them are about the Persian Wars fought in Mesopotamia, two about the Vandal War fought in Africa, three about the Gothic War fought in Italy and Sicily. These seven deal separately with events in the three different regions down to the year 552, when publication was completed, and were followed by one further volume, which covers the events on all fronts down to 554, when the volume was published. Though entitled 'Wars', these volumes contain far more than a narrative of military operations; they provide much material for a general history of the years with which they are concerned. Thus they supply valuable information about important happenings in the capital, such as the terrible insurrection of A.D. 532, and the equally terrible plague that followed ten years later. It is these volumes that are referred to in the footnotes to this translation as Book I, etc.

The second longest work was *Buildings*, an account in six books of the chief architectural splendours with which Justinian enriched the capital down to the year 560. This is a fulsome and tedious work, written in pompous language, and made distasteful by the constant flattery of the imperial pair. Can it be that it was intended to safeguard the writer's position in the eyes of the Emperor, and that it brought him the promotion to which we have referred?

The third work – third in size and in date of publication, but not in date of composition – was *The Secret History*. The two references in this book to the fact that Justinian had so far been ruler for thirty-two years led Gibbon to believe that it was written in A.D. 559. But if we reckon his reign as beginning not in 527 but in 518, since it was not Justin but his nephew who actually governed the Empire, we shall agree with Bury and the other modern scholars who believe the date to have been 550. This seems highly probable in view of the contempt with which Procopius dismisses the earlier monarch as a nonentity. Parallels are not hard to find. When St Luke dates the beginning of the Baptist's ministry as 'the fifteenth year of the reign of Tiberius Caesar' he is almost certainly counting not from that emperor's accession in A.D. 14, but from his association in the imperial prerogatives two years earlier. Eusebius reckons the reign of Augustus as having begun not in 27 or even 31 B.C., but on the Ides of March 44 B.C. Much later the Jacobites were to reckon the years of Charles II's reign not from his restoration in 1660 but from his father's martyrdom eleven years earlier.

In the opening paragraphs of this Introduction we posed

two questions but postponed any attempt to answer them. Why was *The Secret History* written and not published? And why is it so extraordinarily different from the author's other works that some have doubted whether it could have been written by the same man? *The Histories*, which were to win such high commendation from Gibbon, are careful, methodical, chronological, and accurate records of a series of wars, in which tribute is paid to the genius and high character of the commander-in-chief, and no aspersions are cast either on him or his wife or his imperial employers. *The Secret History*, which professes to be an extension of the first seven books of *The Histories*, and begins with sentences which appear to link it with the end of Book VII, is a ferocious diatribe against all four and against many of the Emperor's officials, exposing mercilessly both their public actions and their private lives, and stripping them bare of any claim to admiration or even common respect. From start to finish it is an unpleasant book; some would say horrid. No one who reads it will feel much doubt as to why it was not published. If a fraction of the charges which it levels against the Emperor and Empress are true, imagination boggles at the thought of what would have happened to the author had they ever known that he had written such things about them. The question is not why it was not published but why it was written at all. Was it, as some have suggested, merely a letting off of steam, a boiling over of spleen and spite in a man disgruntled because he was denied promotion? I think not. I believe that knowing that his earlier writings had left much unsaid, though they were truthful and sober history as far as they went and were written in the only way that would make publication possible in a time of tyranny and terror, Procopius felt that the other side of the truth must be set forth too, and expressed with a vehemence and starkness that strike us as extravagant and in bad taste. In his view monstrous crimes must be laid bare with brutal frankness. There must be no pulling of punches.

But even if this is correct, we may still wonder why Procopius should bother to write a book which could not be published. I am satisfied in my own mind that he hoped that it would be published. Surely no sane and successful author, who had published seven books of a history that was acceptable both to the public and to the exalted personages concerned, and who intended to add an eighth book and then go on to write a long treatise on architecture and possibly a work on the affairs of the Church, would waste his time writing a book which unless published would serve no purpose at all, and if published would ensure his own destruction. The book, certainly, could not be published immediately; but Theodora was dead, and if the hated tyrant her husband followed her in a year or two, the book could be published and might well be a triumphant success. Justinian was years older than Procopius, and might reasonably be expected to predecease him by ten or twenty years. Had there ever been an emperor who reigned for nearly half a century and died in his bed at the age of eighty-two? It may well have been that sudden realization of the sad truth that Justinian refused to die provided the reason for his decision to abandon abuse and go to the other extreme, and in writing *Buildings* to lay on flattery with a trowel.

As we have already remarked, the differences between *The Secret History* and the two longer works, so startling at first sight, have led some to deny that they could all be the work of the same writer. These doubts have now been generally abandoned, for careful study reveals that there is no actual contradiction between the different works. No fact is asserted in one and denied in another, though a different complexion is sometimes placed upon the same fact. *The Histories* are full of deserved praise for Belisarius, but no admiration is expressed for his employers, and various hints are dropped that are by no means complimentary to the Emperor. The second work does not unsay any statement in the first. Nor is there any change in the ideas that underlie what is written: the author's attitude to politics, society, and life in general remains unaltered. There is the same prejudice in favour of aristocracy and conservatism. Moreover, a study of the Greek reveals an unmistakable consistency of grammar, vocabulary, and rhythm. No one can read many pages without noticing the constant recurrence of the author's favourite words and phrases, or his addiction to the same rather unusual arrangement of the words. Surely no one would have gone to the trouble of carefully imitating these things for the purpose of passing off as the work of Procopius a book that could not be published.

Similar doubts have been cast on the trustworthiness of the record; but as we have seen, there is no real contradiction between the first work and the second. Procopius himself claimed that his account was 'unvarnished and essentially correct'. Gibbon had no doubts about this, and while criticizing the *tone* of *The Secret History* had no hesitation in reproducing its statements as objectively true, adding the comment, 'Even the most disgraceful facts, some of which had been tenderly hinted at in his public history, are established by their internal evidence, or the authentic monuments of the times.' Monuments and records abound, and while they constantly confirm the statements of Procopius they never subvert them. Only on the ground of incredibility or self-evident falsity can his statements be questioned, and on this matter Gibbon wrote, 'Of these strange Anecdotes a part may be true because probable, and a part true because improbable. Procopius must have *known* the former, and the latter he could scarcely *invent*.' We may add that since Procopius was writing of things almost all of which had happened in the last twenty-five years, the public, or any friends to whom he might have shown the manuscript in secret, would have at once detected any inventions.

Of course the book contains exaggerations, some of which will strike the modern reader as absurd. The author's belief in magic (or was it aphrodisiacs?) and in demon-lovers and demon-emperors, will seem even more absurd; but we must remember that such beliefs were commonly held at the time. So too was the belief that a monarch's wickedness, by provoking the Deity, might bring about floods, earthquakes, and other calamities, which to this day we call 'Acts of God'. A thousand years later the same kind of thing was to be written by John Foxe about Mary Tudor. Again, the book has been denounced as grossly unfair. Of course it is unfair if taken by itself; but to do so is equally unfair. The book should be taken as part of a much larger work, a work in which Procopius puts the pros and cons in different volumes, as another author might put them in different chapters or different paragraphs. First we read of what was achieved by Justinian and his commander in the field. Then we are told that though these men did great things, the one also did a great deal of harm, and his motives were evil; the other lacked moral courage; both were subject to their wives. As regards Belisarius, this is almost the only charge brought against him in *The Secret History*; and it is in reality a tribute to the great man that Procopius suggests that he would never have been overcome by Antonina had she not employed supernatural arts to effect her purpose.

However great the defects of the book may be, there is no denying that for those who wish to know how men lived in other times and places, and are prepared to read of things that were sordid and disgusting, it makes most interesting reading. We find in it not only political and military history, not only scandalous stories, diatribes, and insinuations, but also vivid descriptions of life in that far off age. Byzantium was full of beauty and magnificence, full too of moral and religious corruption. We get an insight into the sad state of the Church, the despicable characters of certain prelates, the criminal methods employed to augment Church funds. We read of a city where sexual morality was apparently non-existent, where adultery and promiscuity were rampant and chastity unknown, where the laws of God and the example of Christ had been forgotten, and the pagan adage 'Let nothing be in excess' had ceased to have a meaning. To read of these things will do us no harm. The only harmful books are those which make wrong seem attractive, or represent sin as being other than the hideous thing that it is. Procopius was unquestionably on the side of right, and the things which are disgusting to us were equally disgusting to him.

Apart from the widespread indifference to religion and

morality, the reader will find in Procopius many things, not all of them objectionable, to remind him of life today. He will read of social services, with State-employed doctors and teachers and subsidized entertainments; of elaborately organized postal services; of espionage and counter-espionage; of rates and taxes, customs-offices, import-duties, and prohibited imports; of defective street lighting and inadequate water-supplies; of monopolies, price-fixing, rake-offs, under-the-counter sales, and the cornering of supplies; of the rising cost of living and depreciation of the currency; of smaller loaves and adulterated flour; of a statute of limitations; of a mad passion for sport and the frantic and aggressive partisanship of its devotees.

It only remains to say something of the literary characteristics of the book, and of its history since it was first mentioned by Suidas.

The work is thought to have been modelled on Theopompus's *History of Philip of Macedon*. Procopius also owed a great deal to Herodotus and Thucydides, particularly the latter, who had set the pattern for *The Histories*, and in language at least influenced the writing of the very dissimilar *Secret History*. He owed little to the Bible, or to Latin authors, but he esteemed highly the great Greek writers of the early and classical periods, such as Homer and Aeschylus, and especially Aristophanes, to four of whose comedies he alludes no less than eight times in this short book. His Greek is excellent, not unlike Attic, though of course the vocabulary had undergone changes, and on the whole lucid, though there are a few difficult passages which translators have interpreted in very different ways. His narrative flows easily, his descriptions are clear, his sentences are not over-long, and the speeches which like all ancient historians he puts into the mouths of his characters are more natural than is sometimes the case.

Mention was made earlier of favourite words that characterize Procopius's style, some twenty of which constantly recur in this book. They are not so conspicuous in a translation, where in accordance with English taste, which demands a more varied vocabulary, they do not always appear in the same guise. But readers of the present version may notice the frequent use of the following – all, always, never, it happened that, manage to, for no reason at all, for the most part. They may also notice that the word 'bishop', which had been in regular use for nearly five centuries, is always replaced by 'archpriest', a word still used in the Orthodox Church.

I need not trouble the reader with a detailed description of the manuscripts. They are few in number and all very late: only two were written as early as the fourteenth century, the rest in the fifteenth and sixteenth, and even the seventeenth and eighteenth. They contain many errors, some of which occur in every single manuscript and are astonishing, for instance 'Romans' for 'Persians', which was correctly given by Suidas.

The first printed edition of *The Secret History* was that of Alemannus, published at Lyons in 1623, with the omission of one section which he thought too indecent for his readers to stomach. This amused Gibbon, who quaintly remarks of Theodora that 'her arts must be veiled in the obscurity of a learned language' and proceeds to quote the passage in the original Greek, adorned with a comment in Latin, adding that the omission was not rectified in the Paris edition (that of Maltretus, 1663). Modern editions include those of Comparetti (Rome, 1898) and Haury (Leipzig, 1913). The last of these is now the standard text. For English readers there is the admirable Loeb Edition, with notes and translation by Dr H. B. Dewing, first issued in 1935. The earliest known English translation was that of Holcroft (1623), the latest an American version by Atwater, which reached our shores in 1963.

I must add a few words about this present translation, which I have tried to make both accurate and readable. For the most part it follows Haury's text, but I have rejected emendations wherever it seemed possible that the MSS might be right. Twice on one page I have refused to admit a 'not' inserted by improvers of the text. I have likewise declined to follow Gibbon and Atwater in changing Theodora's grandson into a nephew without MS authority. Latin words transliterated by Procopius I have retained untranslated, but distinguished by italics: such words as 'praetor' and 'toga' I have treated as English. One Latin word only have I removed altogether – *centenarium*, which denotes the monetary unit employed where large sums were involved. As it is unfamiliar to the great majority of readers, in the eleven passages where it occurs in this book I have converted the sums in question into modern terms, based not on an estimate of purchasing power but on the value of gold. A *centenarium* was undoubtedly a quantity of gold, as Procopius repeatedly states, and all the evidence suggests that it weighed 100 lb. of 12 oz. each. With gold at over £12 10s. 0d. an oz., that would give it a value today of over £15,000, and on that basis I have made my calculations.

The resulting figures must of course be taken as approximate only; but at least they have meaning.

In conclusion, I have resolutely refused to translate *barbaroi* by 'barbarians', and I trust that I have used no other words or expressions savouring of translationese.

Norwich, April 1965

In 1979 the price of gold rose to nearly £165 an ounce. If, therefore, the English equivalents given in the translation are multiplied by twelve the value in modern terms will be roughly indicated.

The purpose of this book

IN recording everything that the Roman people has experienced in successive wars up to the time of writing I have followed this plan – that of arranging all the events described as far as possible in accordance with the actual times and places. But from now on I shall no longer keep to that method: in this volume I shall set down every single thing that has happened anywhere in the Roman Empire. The reason is simple. As long as those responsible for what happened were still alive, it was out of the question to tell the story in the way that it deserved. For it was impossible either to avoid detection by swarms of spies, or if caught to escape death in its most agonizing form. Indeed, even in the company of my nearest relations I felt far from safe. Then again, in the case of many events which in my earlier volumes I did venture to relate I dared not reveal the reasons for what happened. So in this part of my work I feel it my duty to reveal both the events hitherto passed over in silence and the reasons for the events already described.

But as I embark on a new undertaking of a difficult and extraordinarily baffling character, concerned as it is with Justinian and Theodora and the lives they lived, my teeth chatter and I find myself recoiling as far as possible from the task; for I envisage the probability that what I am now about to write will appear incredible and unconvincing to future generations. And again, when in the long course of time the story seems to belong to a rather distant past, I am afraid that I shall be regarded as a mere teller of fairy tales or listed among the tragic poets. One thing, however, gives me confidence to shoulder my heavy task without flinching: my account has no lack of witnesses to vouch for its truth. For my own contemporaries are witnesses fully acquainted with the incidents described, and will pass on to future ages an incontrovertible conviction that these have been faithfully recorded.

And yet there was something else which, when I was all agog to get to work on this volume, again and again held me back for weeks on end. For I inclined to the view that the happiness of our grandchildren would be endangered by my revelations, since it is the deeds of blackest dye that stand in greatest need of being concealed from future generations, rather than they should come to the ears of monarchs as an example to be imitated. For most men in positions of power invariably, through sheer ignorance, slip readily into imitation of their predecessors' vices, and it is to the misdeeds of earlier rulers that they invariably find it easier and less troublesome to turn. But later on I was encouraged to write the story of these events by this reflexion – it will surely be evident to future monarchs that the penalty of their misdeeds is almost certain to overtake them, just as it fell upon the persons described in this book. Then again, their own conduct and character will in turn be recorded for all time; and that will perhaps make them less ready to transgress. For how could the licentious life of Semiramis or the dementia of Sardanapalus and Nero have been known to anyone in later days, if contemporary historians had not left these things on record? Apart from this, those who in the future, if so it happens, are similarly ill used by the ruling powers will not find this record altogether useless; for it is always comforting for those in distress to know that they are not the only ones on whom these blows have fallen.

That is my justification for first recounting the contemptible conduct of Belisarius, and then revealing the equally contemptible conduct of Justinian and Theodora.

CHAPTER I

Belisarius and Antonina

BELISARIUS was married to a woman of whom I had
something to say in the preceding books. Her father and
grandfather were charioteers, who had displayed their skill
in Byzantium and Thessalonica; and her mother was an
actress of easy virtue. She herself in her early years had
lived a profligate kind of life and had thrown off all moral
restraint; she had been continually in the company of her
father's magic-mongering friends, and had learnt the arts
essential to her trade. Later when with all due ceremony
she married Belisarius, she had already given birth to one
child after another. So it was already her intention to be
unfaithful from the start; but she took great care to conceal
this business, not because her own conduct gave her any
qualms, or because she stood in any fear of her spouse – she
never felt the slightest shame for any action whatever, and
thanks to her regular use of magic she could twist her husband round her little finger – but because she dreaded the
vengeance of the Empress; for Theodora was only too
ready to rage at her and bare her teeth.[1] But by assisting her
in matters of exceptional importance she quickly brought
her to heel. The first step was to get rid of Silverius[2] by a
means to be described in a later volume;[3] the second was to

1. Borrowed from Aristophanes' *Peace*.
2. A pope.
3. This volume was apparently never written. Possible Procopius
means 'later in this volume': if so, he neglected to keep this promise.

41

ruin John the Cappadocian, as described already in an earlier
volume.[1] The way was now clear; her fears vanished and
there was no further concealment; she could commit every
crime in the calendar without the slightest hesitation.

The household of Belisarius included a young Thracian
of the name of Theodosius, who had been brought up in the
belief called Eunomianism.[2] On the eve of his voyage to
Libya, Belisarius washed this youngster in the sacred bath,
then lifted him out in his arms, thereby making him the
adopted son of his wife and himself in accordance with the
rules for adoption observed by Christians. From that
moment Antonina, as was to be expected, loved Theodosius,
since the sacred word had made him her son; and she
watched over him with extreme care and kept him under
her wing. Then a little while after she fell madly in love
with him during this voyage, and surrendering herself body
and soul to her passion threw off all fear and respect for the
laws of God and men, and had intercourse with him, at
first in secret but finally before the eyes of domestics of both
sexes. For by now she was helpless against this desire and
unmistakably the slave of her lust, so that she could no
longer see any impediment to its indulgence. Once, in
Carthage, Belisarius surprised them in the very act; yet he
swallowed his wife's lying explanation open-mouthed. He
had found them together in a basement room, and though
he was mad with rage she did not flinch or disguise what
she had done, but merely remarked, 'I came so that the
young man could help me conceal the pick of the spoils
here, in case the Emperor should get to know about them.'

1. Book I.
2. The heresy of Eunomius, a fourth-century bishop of Cyzicus.

This of course was only an excuse, but he seemed satisfied and let the matter drop, though he saw that Theodosius had unfastened the belt holding up the trousers which covered his nakedness. For his passionate love for the woman compelled him to pretend that the evidence of his own eyes was utterly false.

Antonina's profligacy steadily increased till it reached an unimaginable pitch and everybody saw what was going on; but nobody said a word, except a female slave called Macedonia. In Syracuse, when Belisarius had conquered Sicily, this woman made her master swear the most terrible oaths never to betray her to her mistress, and then blurted out to him the whole story, corroborated by the testimony of two lads whose task was to look after the bedroom. On hearing this Belisarius ordered some of his attendants to put Theodosius out of the way. Theodosius, however, heard of this in time and made a dash for Ephesus; for most of Belisarius' attendants, bearing in mind his swiftly changing moods, thought it more expedient to be in the wife's good books than to appear to favour the husband; so they betrayed the instructions then given to them regarding Theodosius.

When Constantine[1] saw how distressed Belisarius was by what had happened, he expressed his complete sympathy, adding the remark, 'If I'd been in your shoes, I should have got rid of the woman rather than the youngster.' When this came to Antonina's ears, she kept her indignation against him secret, waiting for the right moment to display her hatred against him; for she was as malignant as a scorpion and expert at concealing her feelings. A little while later,

1. One of Belisarius's generals.

whether by magic or by cajolement, she convinced her
husband that there was no truth in the girl's accusation; and
he at once invited Theodosius to return, and agreed to hand
over Macedonia and the boys to his wife. She first cut out
the tongues of all three, we are told, then carved them up
into little bits, which she dropped into sacks and threw into
the sea without turning a hair, assisted in all this unholy
business by one of the menservants called Eugenius, the
man who had been instrumental in the monstrous treatment
of Silverius. A little while later Belisarius was persuaded by
his wife to kill Constantine too. For it was at this very time
that the affair of Praesidius and the daggers took place: I
related the whole story in an earlier volume.[1] Constantine
would have been acquitted, but Antonina was inexorable
till he had paid the penalty for the comment which I
recorded a few lines back. By his acquiescence Belisarius
brought on himself the bitter hostility of the Emperor and
of the influential Romans one and all. So ended that chapter
of the story.

Theodosius, however, sent word that he would be unable
to come to Italy, where Belisarius and Antonina were making a stay at the time, unless Photius[2] were got out of the way.
For Photius was temperamentally quick to take offence if
anyone else had more influence than himself in any quarter
whatever. But in the case of Theodosius and his friends he
had ample excuse for choking with rage: he himself, though
he was a son, found himself counting for nothing, while his
rival enjoyed great power and was becoming immensely
wealthy. It is said that at Carthage and Ravenna he had pur-

1. Book VI.
2. Son of Antonina by a previous husband.

loined no less than £1,500,000[1] from the two palaces, which he was privileged to administer on his own responsibility and with full powers. When Antonina learnt of Theodosius's refusal, she made persistent attempts to trap the boy, and pursued him with murderous plots until she succeeded in forcing him to leave Italy and proceed to Byzantium, as he could no longer risk falling into her traps, and in persuading Theodosius to join her in Italy. There she gained unlimited enjoyment from the company of her lover and the blindness of her husband, and a little later she returned to Byzantium escorted by them both.

In the capital Theodosius was in an agony of fear through the knowledge of his guilt, and his mind was distracted. He saw no possibility at all of averting suspicion, as he realized that Antonina could no longer keep her passion out of sight or give vent to it in secret, but was perfectly happy to be an avowed adulteress and to be spoken of as such. So he again betook himself to Ephesus, and adopting the customary tonsure had himself enrolled amongst the 'monks'. At this Antonina became completely demented, and changing her dress and her whole manner of life to the style of those in mourning she wandered continually about the house, wailing, shrieking, and lamenting even in the presence of her husband. What a treasure she had lost; how faithful, how winning, how kind, how alive! Finally she even dragged her husband into these lamentations and made him join in. Anyway, the unfortunate man began weeping and crying aloud for his beloved Theodosius! Later he even approached the Emperor, appealing both to him and to the Empress, till he persuaded them to fetch Theodosius back,

1. See Introduction, p. 34.

as he was indispensable to his domestic life and always would be. Theodosius, however, flatly refused to leave Ephesus, insisting that he was determined to give unswerving obedience to the monastic discipline. This was a downright lie; the moment Belisarius left Byzantium he planned to join Antonina surreptitiously.

And join her he did; for very soon Belisarius, accompanied by Photius, was on his way to resume hostilities against Chosroes. But Antonina stayed behind, a thing she had never done before: to prevent her husband from being alone and coming to his senses, and from treating her magic with contempt and seeing her for what she was, it was her invariable custom to accompany him to all parts of the world. And in order that Theodosius might be able to resume his association with her, she was impatient to get Photius out of the way. To this end she urged some of her husband's staff to torment and insult him continually, never missing an opportunity; while she herself wrote almost every day, pouring out slanders in an endless stream and making the boy the target for every weapon. Under this treatment Photius perforce resolved to use slander against his mother; and when a man arrived from Byzantium with the news that Theodosius was secretly staying with Antonina, he at once took him into Belisarius' presence, adjuring him to tell the whole story.

When Belisarius learned the truth, he was beside himself with fury, and prostrated himself before Photius's feet and implored the boy to avenge him, monstrously ill used as he was by those from whom he least expected it. 'My precious boy,' he cried, 'you have no idea what your father was like; for you were only an infant in arms when he departed this life, leaving you nothing at all: he was not overblest with this world's goods. It was I who brought you up, though I am only your stepfather: now you've reached an age when it is your duty to defend me with might and main if I am wronged; and you have risen to the rank of consul and have amassed so much wealth that I might be called your father and every other kind of relation, my good fellow, as to all intents and purposes I am. For it is not by community of blood but by mutual kindness that people habitually measure their affection for each other. The time has come when you must no longer allow me, besides the wrecking of my marriage, to be stripped as well of possessions on so vast a scale, or your own mother to bring upon herself universal and utter contempt. And remember that the sins of women do not fall on their husbands only: they do still more damage to their children, whose misfortune it will almost certainly be to incur a reputation for having a natural resemblance in character to their mothers. You must realize too that this is the position with me: I love my wife dearly, and if I get the chance to give the wrecker of my marriage his deserts I shall do her no harm; but while Theodosius is alive I can never forgive her for what she is accused of.'

In reply to this Photius agreed to give all the help he could, though he was afraid it might cost him dear: he had precious little confidence in his stepfather's swiftly changing moods towards his wife; for a great many things worried him, especially what had happened to Macedonia. In view of this the two swore to each other all the most terrible oaths that are in use among Christians and are recognized as such, pledging themselves never to leave each other in the lurch,

even in situations of the most desperate danger. To make
the attempt then and there struck them as inadvisable; but
when Antonina arrived from Byzantium and Theodosius
went to Ephesus, that would be the moment for Photius to
appear in Ephesus and take possession both of Theodosius
and of the money with the minimum of trouble. Now at
this very time when they had launched their all-out attack
on Persian territory, the incident involving John the Cappadocian happened to be taking place in Byzantium, as I
explained in an earlier volume.[1] In that account, I confess,
fear led me to suppress one fact. The deception of John and
his daughter by Antonina was no casual occurrence: it was
backed by a multitude of oaths, the most terrible form
of declaration in Christian eyes, assuring them that no
treachery was purposed towards them. When her object
had been achieved and she felt much more secure in the
affections of the Empress, she dispatched Theodosius to
Ephesus, while she herself, anticipating no difficulty, set out
for the East. Belisarius had just captured the fortress of
Sisauranon when someone informed him of her imminent
arrival. He instantly dismissed everything else from his
mind and withdrew his forces. It happened that, as I made
clear in my earlier account, certain other events which had
taken place in the Roman camp disposed him to retreat at
this time. But the information now received induced him
to take this step much more precipitately. As I stated, however, in the first paragraph of this book, at that time I judged
it too dangerous to disclose all the reasons for what had
occurred.

   The result of this move was that an accusation was levelled

   1. Book II.

48

at Belisarius by Romans everywhere of having sacrificed
the most vital interests of the State to his own domestic
concerns. For at the start he had been so incapacitated by
his wife's waywardness that he positively refused to go
thus far beyond the bounds of the Roman Empire, determined as he was that the moment he learnt that his wife had
arrived from Byzantium he must be able to turn back and
catch and punish her then and there. To this end he ordered
Arethas and his men to cross the River Tigris; but they
effected nothing to speak of and were soon on their way
home, while he himself was careful not to go even a day's
march beyond the Roman frontier. The fortress of Sisauranon, even for a lightly equipped traveller, is certainly
more than a day's journey[1] from the limits of Roman territory if he goes via the city of Nisibis; but there is another
route which is only half as long. And yet if he had been
prepared from the first to cross the Tigris with his entire
army, I have no doubt that he would have despoiled the
whole Assyrian region, gone right on to the city of
Ctesiphon without meeting any resistance at all, freed the
prisoners from Antioch[2] and any other Romans who happened to be there, and then returned safely to his fatherland.
Then again it was mainly his fault that Chosroes met no
real opposition on the way back from Colchis. How this
happened I will explain at once.

When Chosroes, son of Cabades, invaded the territory
of Colchis and won the successes which I recorded in an
earlier volume,[3] including the capture of Petra,[4] the Persian

1. Twenty-four miles, as Procopius tells us elsewhere.
2. Chosroes had taken Antioch in A.D. 540.   3. Book II.
4. In Colchis; not the famous city in Arabia.

army suffered heavy casualties both in the actual fighting
and in negotiating the difficult country. As I pointed out
in that volume, roads are almost non-existent in Lazica
and precipices abound on every side. As if that was not
enough, an epidemic swept through the army and most of
the soldiers died, while many of the survivors perished for
want of necessary food. At this crisis too persons arriving
there from Persia brought the news that Belisarius had
defeated Nabedes in battle near Nisibis and was now
advancing; that he had stormed Sisauranon and taken Bleschames prisoner with eight hundred Persian cavalry; that
he had dispatched another Roman force under Arethas the
Saracen commander; and that this force had crossed the
Tigris and plundered the whole countryside, which till then
had remained unravaged. It happened too that Chosroes
had sent a column of Huns against the Armenians who
were Roman subjects, in the hope that the Romans in that
locality would be so busy dealing with this threat that they
would be oblivious to events in Lazica. Other messengers
now brought word that these Huns had been intercepted
by Valerian and his Romans: they had joined battle with
them and had been severely worsted in the encounter, the
column being almost wiped out.

The Persians had suffered untold misery in Lazica, and
they were apprehensive lest during their retreat they should
run into some enemy force in the narrow defiles and dense
thickets, and in their sorry disarray perish to a man. When
they heard of the latest disaster they were alarmed by the
danger to their wives and children and to their homeland.
The more responsible members of the invading army began
to protest vehemently to Chosroes, accusing him of violat-

ing both his own oaths and international laws accepted by all nations: in time of peace he had invaded Roman territory entirely without provocation, and he was guilty of aggression against a state that had stood the test of time and was superior to all others, capable of withstanding all his armed onslaughts.

There was imminent danger of mutiny, and Chosroes, seriously alarmed, attempted to cure the distemper with the following remedy. He read aloud to them a letter which the Empress happened to have written to Zaberganes a little while before. The contents were as follows:

What an impression you made on me, Zaberganes, by your evident regard for our interests, you saw for yourself a little while back, when you came as an ambassador to our court. My high opinion of you would be confirmed if you were to induce King Chosroes to pursue a peaceful policy towards our State. In that case I can guarantee that you will reap a handsome reward from my husband, who would not think of taking any action whatever without my approval.

When Chosroes had read this aloud, he took to task any of the leading Persians who imagined that any state worth the name was run by a woman. He managed thus to stem the violence of the men's hostility; but even so he was very apprehensive as he marched away, fully expecting to find his route blocked by the forces of Belisarius. Not a single enemy, however, appeared in his path, and to his great relief he got back safely to his own domains.

On reaching Roman territory Belisarius found that his wife had arrived from Byzantium. He kept her under guard in disgrace, and made repeated moves to get rid of her altogether. But he always relented, overcome, it seems to me, by red-hot passion. Rumour has it also that his wife used magic arts to enslave him, instantly destroying his resolution. Meanwhile Photius set off post haste for Ephesus, taking with him one of the eunuchs, Calligonus by name, who served as procurer to his mistress. He had put the man in fetters, and on the journey he tortured him till he disclosed all Antonina's secrets. Theodosius, forewarned, took sanctuary in the Church of John the Apostle, the most sacred shrine in Ephesus and one held in special honour. But Andrew, the Archpriest of Ephesus, accepted a bribe and handed him over to his pursuer.

Meanwhile Theodora, who had heard all that had befallen Antonina and was anxious for her safety, ordered Belisarius to bring her to Byzantium. Photius on learning this sent Theodosius into Cilicia, where the picked spearmen and footguards happened to be quartered for the winter, instructing the escort to convey the prisoner with the utmost stealth, and on arrival in Cilicia to keep him in an absolutely safe place of confinement, giving no one a chance to discover his whereabouts. He himself, accompanied by Calligonus, took Theodosius's money, amounting to a very considerable sum, to Byzantium. There the Empress was demonstrating to the world that she knew how to repay bloody favours with bigger and more polluted gifts. Antonina had recently entrapped a single enemy, the Cappadocian, and betrayed him to Theodora: Theodora handed over a small army of men to Antonina, and without preferring a charge brought them to destruction. Some of the close friends of Belisarius and Photius she subjected to physical tortures, even though she had nothing against them except their friendship with these two men, and disposed of in such a way that even now we do not know what happened to them in the end. Others too she charged with the same offence and sentenced to be deported. One of the men who had accompanied Photius to Ephesus, Theodosius by name, though he had been honoured with membership of the Senate, she deprived of his property and threw into a dungeon, where he was forced to stand in pitch darkness, his neck tied to a manger with a noose so small that it was always pulled tight round his throat and never for a moment hung loose. And so the poor fellow stood continuously at this manger, eating and sleeping and performing all other natural functions; and he resembled an ass in every particular short of braying. Four months, no less, he passed in this sort of existence, until he was overcome by sick melancholy and went stark mad; then at last he was released from his prison, and promptly died.

Theodora also compelled Belisarius, much against his inclination, to lay aside his quarrel with his wife Antonina. Photius she subjected to one servile torture after another, tearing the flesh off his back and shoulders with merciless flogging, insisting that he should disclose the whereabouts of Theodosius and the procurer. But Photius, despite the torment that he was enduring, was determined to keep his sworn word, though he was of feeble constitution and had been a loose liver in his youth, and had always attended to his physical comfort with the greatest care, while rough treatment and hardship were unknown to him. Anyway, Photius gave away none of Belisarius's secrets; later, however, all the facts hitherto concealed came to light. The Empress also found Calligonus there and passed him over to Antonina. Next she summoned Theodosius to Byzantium, and when he arrived she for the moment concealed him in the Palace: next day she sent for Antonina and said, 'Dearest Patrician, a pearl fell into my hands yesterday, the most beautiful that has ever been seen. If you wish, I shall not grudge you the sight of it, but will show it to you.' Antonina, who did not grasp the purport of all this, begged and besought the Empress to show her the pearl. Whereupon Theodosius was produced from the chamber of one of the eunuchs and shown to her. Antonina was so overcome with joy that at first she was too delighted to say a word; then she acknowledged that Theodora had showered favours upon her, and hailed her as Protectress and Benefactress and Mistress indeed. This Theodosius the Empress detained in the Palace, surrounding him with luxury and pleasures of every kind, and swearing that she would make him a general in the Roman army in the near future. But justice of a sort forestalled her: he had an attack of dysentery, and that was the end of him.

Theodora had secret chambers completely hidden from view, pitch-dark and isolated, where night and day were indistinguishable. There she imprisoned Photius and kept him guarded for a long time. From this prison he had the extraordinary luck to escape twice over and get clear. The first time he took refuge in the Church of the Mother of God, which the Byzantines consider most sacred – the name that was actually given to it – and sat down in front of the holy table as a suppliant.

From there Theodora removed him by brute force, and sent him back to his prison. The second time he went to the Church of Sophia[1] and before anyone could stop him he

1. Not a saint, but Wisdom.

actually sat down in the baptismal tank, which Christians at all times reverence more than anything else. But even from there the woman was able to drag him: there was not one inviolable spot that ever remained beyond her reach; and in her eyes violence done to sacred things of any and every kind was nothing at all. And like the common people the Christian priests were so terrified of her that they left the way clear and allowed her to do as she liked. So it was that Photius spent no less than three years in this kind of existence; but afterwards the prophet Zechariah stood over him in a dream and, it is said, commanded him to flee, solemnly promising to assist him in this endeavour. Convinced by this vision he broke out of his prison and made his way to Jerusalem without being caught; for though thousands were on the look-out for him, not a single person recognized him even after meeting him face to face. In Jerusalem he adopted the tonsure and arrayed himself in the habit of a 'monk', managing thus to escape Theodora's vengeance.

Belisarius, on the other hand, had paid no regard to his oaths and had chosen to give no help at all to his stepson, though he was being treated in the abominable way that I have described. So it is not surprising that in all his subsequent undertakings he found the hand of God against him. For no sooner had he been dispatched against Chosroes and his Persians, who had for the third time invaded Roman territory, than he laid himself open to a charge of cowardice. He did indeed appear to have won a notable success in that he had shaken off the war from that region; but when Chosroes crossed the River Euphrates, captured the teeming city of Callinicus without meeting any resistance, and enslaved tens of thousands of Romans, Belisarius did not bother even to pursue the enemy, leaving people to think that one of two things must be true: he had hung back either through wilful neglect of his duty or through sheer cowardice.

It was not long before Belisarius suffered another blow. The epidemic which I recorded in an earlier volume[1] was taking heavy toll of the people in Byzantium. Among those attacked was the Emperor Justinian, who became very ill indeed; it was even stated that he was dead. This story was spread about by rumour and carried right to the Roman camp. There some of the officers declared that if the Romans set up someone else in Byzantium as emperor over them, they would never submit to him. But the unexpected happened, and before long the Emperor recovered; thereupon the officers of the army flung accusations at each other. Peter the general and John, nicknamed 'The Guzzler', insisted that they had heard Belisarius and Buzes talking in the way I have just mentioned. These criticisms, the Empress Theodora alleged, had been directed by their authors against herself, and she could not contain her indignation. She instantly recalled them all to Byzantium, and held an inquiry into the report. Then without notice she summoned Buzes to her private apartment as if to consult him on some matter of the first importance.

There was a system of cellars beneath the Palace, secure and labyrinthine, and suggestive of hell itself. In these she habitually kept under lock and key any who had incurred her displeasure. Into this hole Buzes was flung in his turn;

1. Book II. The date was A.D. 542.

and there, though the descendant of consuls, he remained,
for ever oblivious of the passage of time. For as he sat in
darkness he could not himself make out whether it was day
or night, and he was never allowed to speak to anyone else.
The man who tossed him his daily ration of food met him
as beast meets beast, neither saying a word. Everyone took it
for granted that he had died at once, but to mention his
name or say a word about him was more than anyone dared
to do. Two years and four months later Theodora took pity
on her prisoner and set him free. Everybody stared at him
as if he had come back from the dead. For the rest of his life
the unfortunate man suffered from bad eyesight, and his
general health was very feeble.

Such was the treatment meted out to Buzes. Belisarius,
although none of the charges was brought home to him,
was at the instigation of the Empress deprived by the
Emperor of the command which he held, and replaced by
Martin as general in the East. Belisarius's picked spearmen
and footguards, together with those of his personal attendants who were trained fighting men, were, on the Emperor's
instructions, to be divided up between some of the officers
and Palace eunuchs. These drew lots for them and shared
them, arms and all, among themselves, as each man happened to be lucky. Many of his friends and other old helpers
were forbidden to associate with Belisarius any more. A
pitiful sight and an incredible spectacle, Belisarius went
about as a private citizen in Byzantium, almost alone,
always gloomy and melancholy, in continual fear of death
by a murderer's hand. Learning that he had accumulated
great wealth in the East, the Empress sent one of the Palace
eunuchs to bring it all to her.

Antonina, as I have said, had fallen out with her husband, but was an inseparable friend of the Empress because she had recently contrived to ruin John the Cappadocian. So the Empress, determined to gratify Antonina, did all in her power to make it seem that it was thanks to his wife's intercessions that the husband had been spared and saved from his calamitous position, and to arrange matters so that Antonina should not only be completely reconciled with her unfortunate husband, but should unmistakably be his rescuer as if she had saved a prisoner of war. It happened in this way. Early one morning Belisarius came to the Palace, escorted as usual by a few poor specimens of humanity. He found their Majesties anything but friendly, and into the bargain was grossly insulted there by some vulgar scoundrels. It was late in the evening when he set off for home, and on the way back he repeatedly turned round and looked in every possible direction from which he might see his would-be murderers coming towards him. In the grip of this terror he went upstairs to his bedroom and sat down on the bed alone. There was no one honourable thought in his head; he was not conscious that he had once been a man. The sweat ran down his face unceasingly; his head swam; his whole body trembled in an agony of despair, tormented as he was by slavish fears and craven anxieties utterly unworthy of a man.

Antonina, as if she was quite unaware of what was afoot and had no inkling of anything that was to happen, was walking endlessly about the room to relieve an alleged attack of heartburn; for they still eyed each other suspiciously. Meanwhile a man called Quadratus arrived from the Palace when it was already dark, passed through the outer gateway, and appeared without warning outside the door of the men's apartments, and announced that the Empress had sent him there. When Belisarius heard this, he drew up his hands and feet on the bed and lay motionless on his back, convinced that his time had come; so completely had every spark of manhood deserted him. Without waiting to get near him Quadratus held up a letter from the Empress for him to see. It read as follows:

How you have behaved towards us, my good sir, you know only too well. But I personally owe so much to your wife that for her sake I have resolved to dismiss all the charges brought against you, making her a present of your life. So from now on you need have no fear for either your life or your money. How you regard your wife your future conduct will show us.

When Belisarius had read the letter through, he was beside himself with joy and longed at the same time to show then and there how he felt. So he sprang up at once, threw himself on his face at his wife's feet, and flung his arms round both her knees. Then raining kisses on each ankle in turn he declared that he owed his life entirely to her, and swore that henceforth he would be her faithful slave, not her husband. Of his money the Empress gave gold to the value of £450,000 to the Emperor, and returned the balance to Belisarius.

Such was the downfall of Belisarius the general, to whom fortune a little while before had presented Gelimer and Vittigis¹ as prisoners of war. But for a long time both Justinian and Theodora had been bitterly jealous of the man's wealth: it was far too great, and more suited to the

1. Kings respectively of the Vandals and Visigoths.

court of an emperor. They maintained that he had spirited away the bulk of the money in the public treasuries of Gelimer and Vittigis, handing over a tiny and quite negligible fraction of it to the Emperor. But the toils Belisarius had undergone and the execration they would bring upon themselves could not be disregarded; nor could they devise any convincing excuse for taking action against him. So they bided their time. But now that the Empress had caught him in a state of abject terror and completely cowed, a single stroke sufficed to make her mistress of his entire property. For a marriage-connexion was promptly established between them by the union of Joannina, the only child of Belisarius, with Anastasius, the son of the Empress's daughter.[1] Belisarius now asked to be restored to his proper position and appointed Commander-in-Chief, in the East, so that he could again lead the Roman army against Chosroes and the Persians. But Antonina would not hear of it: in that part of the world, she insisted, she had been grossly insulted by him, and he should never see it again.

And so Belisarius was appointed Commander of the Imperial Grooms, and for the second time he set out for Italy, after giving the Emperor an undertaking, it is said, that he would never ask him for money during this campaign, but would himself pay for all the necessary equipment out of his own pocket. It was universally surmised that Belisarius settled the problem of his wife in this way, and gave the Emperor the undertaking described above regarding the forthcoming campaign, simply with the object of getting away from life in Byzantium; and that the moment

1. The grandmother of this marriageable young man was only about forty, unless Procopius has antedated the betrothal.

he found himself outside the city walls he would instantly resort to arms and plunge into some gallant and heroic enterprise in order to score off his wife and those who had humiliated him. Belisarius, however, paid no heed to anything that had happened: completely oblivious and indifferent to the oaths which he had sworn to Photius and all his most intimate friends, he went where his wife directed him; for he was hopelessly in love with her, though she was already a woman of sixty.[1]

But when he arrived in Italy, there was not a single day when things went right for him, because the hand of God was unmistakably against him. At first, it is true, the plans which in the circumstances he devised for dealing with Theudatus and Vittigis, though apparently unsuited to his purpose, for the most part brought about the desired result; but in the later stages, despite the reputation which he gained for having planned his campaign on sound lines as a result of the experience gained in dealing with the problems of this war, his ill success in the sequel was for the most part put down to apparent errors of judgement. So true is it that it is not our own devices that control our lives, but the power of God – the thing which we too often refer to as chance, simply because we do not know what makes events follow the course we see them follow. When there seems to be no reason for a thing it is almost inevitably put down to chance. But this is a question on which opinions may reasonably differ.

So it was that after coming to Italy a second time Belisarius returned home utterly discredited. For, as I explained in an earlier volume,[2] in spite of five years' effort he never once

1. Her husband was only thirty-nine.   2. Book VII.

succeeded in disembarking on any part of the coast, unless
there was a fortress handy: the whole of that time he sailed
about, trying one landing-place after another. Totila[1] was
desperate to catch him outside a protecting wall; but he
failed to make contact, as Belisarius himself and the entire
Roman army were in the grip of panic fear, with the result
that he not only failed to recover a yard of lost ground but
actually lost Rome as well, and very nearly everything else.
At the same time he devoted himself heart and soul to the
pursuit of wealth and the unlimited acquisition of illicit
gain, on the plea that he had not received a penny from the
Emperor. In fact, he plundered indiscriminately nearly all
the Italians who lived at Ravenna or in Sicily and anyone
else he could reach, pretending that he was making them
pay the penalty of their misdeeds. Thus he even went for
Herodian,[2] demanding money from him and using
every possible means to terrorize him. This so infuriated
Herodian that he turned his back on the Roman army and
at once put himself, the units under his command, and
the town of Spolitium in the hands of Totila and the
Goths.

How Belisarius came to quarrel with Vitalian's nephew
John, thereby doing untold damage to the Roman cause,
is the next question that I must answer.

Such savage enmity against Germanus had the Empress
conceived – enmity of which she made no secret at all – that
although he was the Emperor's nephew no one dared marry
into his family, and his sons remained single until their best

1. A Goth who was elected king in A.D. 541, overran most of
Italy and Sicily, but in 552 was defeated and killed by Narses.
2. A Roman commander.

years had gone.¹ His daughter Justina, too though she was a mature woman of eighteen, was still without a bridegroom. Consequently when John was dispatched by Belisarius on an errand to Byzantium, Germanus was compelled to negotiate with him on the subject of a marriage with her, despite the fact that John's rank was far inferior to his own. As the suggestion appealed to them both, they agreed to bind each other by the most terrible oaths that they would do everything in their power to effect the proposed union; for each of them profoundly distrusted the other, the one being aware that he was reaching far beyond his rank, the other having no other hope of a son-in-law.

This was more than the Empress could bear. Putting all scruples aside, she went for them both with every available weapon and without hesitation, in her determination to bring their plans to nothing. When all her efforts at intimidation produced no effect on either of them, she announced in so many words that she would destroy John. In consequence, when John was again dispatched to Italy, he dared not go anywhere near Belisarius for fear of Antonina's machinations, until that lady was safely back in Byzantium. For there was every reason to suspect that the Empress had entrusted her with the task of arranging his murder; and as John weighed Antonina's character and reminded himself that Belisarius let his wife have her own way in everything, he was seized with uncontrollable fear. Is it to be wondered at that Roman authority, already on its last legs, collapsed completely?

This then is how the Gothic War went for Belisarius. Despairing of success, he appealed to the Emperor for per-

1. Or *as long as the Empress was alive.* The Greek is doubtful.

mission to leave Italy forthwith. When he learnt that Justinian was agreeable to his request he was delighted and set off immediately for home, leaving the Roman army and the Italians to take care of themselves. Most of the country he left in enemy hands, while the beleaguered city of Perusia was in such a desperate plight that before his journey was completed it was taken by storm and experienced every horror imaginable, as I recorded in full long ago.[1] At the same time a heavy blow fell upon his own household, as we shall see next.

The Empress Theodora, impatient to secure the betrothal of Belisarius's daughter to her own grandson, wrote letter after letter to the girl's parents, worrying them to death. They, in their anxiety to prevent the alliance, sought to postpone the marriage till they themselves returned, and when summoned to Byzantium by the Empress pleaded that they could not leave Italy just then. But she had set her heart on making her grandson master of Belisarius's wealth, knowing that it would all go to the girl, as Belisarius had no other child. She put no trust, however, in the intentions of Antonina, and was afraid that when she herself departed from the scene Antonina would show no loyalty towards the imperial house, although Theodora had treated her so generously when she was in great difficulties, but would tear up the contract. And so, in defiance of all morality, she made the immature girl live with the boy in unlawful union. It is said that by secret pressure she actually forced her, though most unwilling, to have intercourse with him, and when in this way the girl had lost her virginity, arranged for her to marry him, for fear the Emperor might put a stop to her

1. Book VII.

little game. However, when the deed was done, a burning love for each other took possession of Anastasius and his child bride, and they spent eight whole months together in blissful union.[1]

But when death removed the Empress, Antonina came to Byzantium, and wilfully oblivious of the favours Theodora had so recently bestowed on her, paid no regard at all to the fact that if she married the girl to anyone else, she would be regarded as an ex-prostitute. She had no use for Theodora's offspring as a son-in-law, and although the girl was unwilling in the extreme she compelled her to part from the man she adored. By this action she won a universal reputation for utter heartlessness; and yet when her husband arrived she had no difficulty at all in persuading him to share the responsibility with her for this abominable outrage.

This, then, was the moment when the man's character was laid bare for all to see. It is true that when on an earlier occasion he had given his sworn word to Photius and some of his closest friends, and then had shamelessly broken it, he had been forgiven by everyone. For the cause of his faithlessness, they suspected, was not his subservience to his wife but his fear of the Empress. But when, as I remarked, death removed Theodora, he paid no regard either to Photius or any other of those nearest to him, but allowed it to be seen that his wife was mistress over him, and Calligonus her procurer was master. Then at last he was repudiated by everyone, was made the target for endless gossip, and was dismissed with contempt as a hopeless fool.

1. This story seems inconsistent with the statement that Antonina was sixty years old.

Such, then, is the record – unvarnished and essentially correct – of the misdeeds of Belisarius. Let us turn now to those committed in Libya by Sergius, son of Bacchus, of which I gave an adequate account in the appropriate place,[1] showing that he did more than anyone to destroy Roman authority in that region; for he not only treated with contempt the oaths which he had sworn on the Gospels to the Leuathae, but even put the eighty ambassadors to death without the slightest pretext. Only one addition need now be made to my account, namely that these men had no sinister motive in coming to Sergius, and Sergius had no excuse for suspecting them: he pledged his word to them, invited them to dinner, and put them to death in the most dastardly manner. It was this outrage that brought about the destruction of Solomon and the Roman army, and of all the Libyans; for on his account, especially after the death of Solomon which I recorded earlier, not an officer nor a private was prepared to face the hazards of war. Worst of all, John son of Sisinniolus was so furious with him that he kept clear of the fighting till Areobindus arrived in Libya. For Sergius was soft and unwarlike, in character and development quite immature, a helpless slave to envy and boastfulness towards everyone, ostentatious in his way of life and blown up with pride. But, as it happened, he had become a suitor for the grand-daughter of Antonina, Belisarius's wife; so the Empress absolutely declined to punish him in any way or to deprive him of his command, although she saw that the ruin of Libya was proceeding apace: with the full approval of the Emperor she even allowed Sergius's brother Solomon, the murderer of Pegasius,

1. Book IV.

to go scot-free. How that happened I will speedily make
clear.

When Pegasius had ransomed Solomon from the Leuathae and the tribe had gone back home, Solomon, along
with Pegasius his ransomer and a handful of soldiers, set out
for Carthage. On the way Pegasius caught Solomon committing an offence of some sort, and remarked with considerable emphasis that he ought not to forget how a short
time before God had rescued him from the enemy. Solomon,
thinking that he had been sneered at for letting himself be
taken prisoner, lost his temper and killed Pegasius on the
spot – a poor return to the man who had saved him. When
Solomon arrived in Byzantium, the Emperor acquitted him
of the murder on the ground that he had executed a traitor
to the Roman Empire. He furthermore gave him a letter
ensuring his immunity from any proceedings in this matter.
Having thus escaped punishment Solomon went off in great
glee to the East, to visit his birthplace and his family at home.
But punishment at the hand of God overtook him on the
way and removed him from human sight. So much for the
story of Solomon and Pegasius.

CHAPTER 2

Justin, Justinian, and Theodora

WHAT sort of people were Justinian and Theodora? and how did it come about that they destroyed the greatness of Rome? These are the questions that I must answer next.

When Leon occupied the imperial throne of Byzantium, three young farmers of Illyrian origin, Zimarchus, Dityvistus, and Justin who came from Vederiana, had been waging an endless war at home with all that poverty meant. So they determined to get away from it all and went off to join the army. They covered the whole distance to Byzantium on foot, carrying on their own shoulders cloaks in which on their arrival they had nothing but dry biscuits dropped in before they left home. Their names were entered in the army lists, and the Emperor picked them out to serve in the Palace Guard, as they were all men of exceptional physique.

Some time later when Anastasius had succeeded to the imperial power, he was involved in war with the Isaurians, who had taken up arms against him. He sent an army of considerable size to deal with them, the commander being John the Hunchback. This John had locked up Justin in prison because of some misdemeanour, intending to dispatch him on the following day. This he would have done but for a dream-vision which came to him in time to prevent it. The general said that in a dream he was confronted by a being of colossal size, too powerful in every way to be taken for a man. This being commanded him to release the

68

man whom he had that day imprisoned: he himself on waking from sleep dismissed the vision from his mind. But when the next night came, he dreamt that he again heard the same words as before, but remained just as unwilling to carry out the order. Then for the third time the vision stood over him, threatening total ruin unless he did as he was told, and adding that one day he would be in a great rage, and then he would need this man and his family.

This occurrence enabled Justin to survive his immediate danger; and as time went on he acquired great power. The Emperor Anastasius gave him command of the Palace Guards; and when he himself passed from the scene, Justin on the strength of this command succeeded to the throne, though he was by now a doddering old man, totally illiterate – in popular parlance, he didn't know his A B C – an unheard-of thing in a Roman. It was the invariable custom that the Emperor should append his own signature to all documents embodying decrees drafted by him. Justin, however, was incapable of either drafting his own decrees or taking an intelligent interest in the measures contemplated: the official whose luck it was to be his chief adviser – a man called Proclus, who held the rank of 'Quaestor' – used to decide all measures as he himself thought fit. But to secure authority for these in the Emperor's own handwriting the men responsible for this business proceeded as follows. On a short strip of polished wood they cut a stencil in the shape of four letters spelling the Latin for I HAVE READ.[1] Then they used to dip a pen in the special ink reserved for emperors and place it in the hands of the Emperor Justin. Next they took the strip of wood described above and laid it on the

1. *LEGI.*

document, grasped the Emperor's hand, and while he held the pen guided it along the pattern of the four letters, taking it round all the bends cut in the wooden stencil. Then away they went, carrying the Emperor's writing, such as it was.

That was the kind of emperor the Romans had in Justin. He was married to a woman called Lupicina, a foreign slave who had previously been purchased by another man and had become his concubine. But in the evening of her days she became joint ruler with Justin of the Roman Empire. Justin was not capable of doing any harm to his subjects or any good either. He was uncouth in the extreme, utterly inarticulate and incredibly boorish. His nephew Justinian, though still quite young, used to manage all the affairs of state, and he brought on the Romans disasters which surely surpassed both in gravity and in number all that had ever been heard of at any period of history. For without the slightest hesitation he used to embark on the inexcusable murdering of his fellow-men and the plundering of other people's property; and it did not matter to him how many thousands lost their lives, although they had given him no provocation whatever. The maintenance of established institutions meant nothing to him: endless innovations were his constant preoccupation. In a word, he was a unique destroyer of valuable institutions.

The plague, as I mentioned in an earlier volume,[1] fell upon the whole world; yet just as many people escaped as had the misfortune to succumb – either because they escaped the infection altogether, or because they got over it if they happened to be infected. But this man not a single person in the whole Roman Empire could escape: like any

1. Book II.

other visitation from heaven falling on the entire human
race he left no one completely untouched. Some he killed
without any justification; others he reduced to penury,
making them even more wretched than those who had
died. In fact, they begged him to put an end to their misery,
by any death however painful. Some he deprived of their
possessions and of life as well. But it gave him no satisfaction
merely to ruin the Roman Empire: he insisted on making
himself master of Libya and Italy for the sole purpose of
destroying their inhabitants along with those already subject
to him. He had not been ten days in office before he executed
Amantius, controller of the Palace eunuchs, with several
others, for no reason at all, charging him with nothing
more than an injudicious remark about John, the archpriest
of the city. This outrage made him more feared than any
man alive. His next step was to send for the pretender
Vitalian, whose safety he had previously guaranteed by
taking part with him in the Christian sacraments. But a
little later Justinian took offence through groundless suspicion, and put him to death in the Palace along with his
closest friends without the slightest justification, making no
attempt to honour his pledges, the most solemn imaginable.

The people have long been divided into two factions, as I
explained in an earlier volume.[1] Justinian attached himself
to one of them, the Blues, to whom he had already given
enthusiastic support, and so contrived to produce universal
chaos. By doing so he brought the Roman State to its knees.
However, not all the Blues were prepared to follow the lead
of Justinian, but only the militant partisans. Yet even these,

1. Book I.

71

as things went from bad to worse, appeared to be the most self-disciplined of men; for the licence given them went far beyond the misdemeanours which they actually committed. Needless to say, the Green partisans did not stay quiet either: they too pursued an uninterrupted career of crime, as far as they were permitted, although at every moment one or other was paying the penalty. As a result they were constantly provoked to commit crimes far more audacious still; for when people are unfairly treated they naturally turn to desperate courses. So now that he was fanning the flames and openly spurring on the Blues, the entire Roman Empire was shaken to the foundations as if an earthquake or a cataclysm had struck it, or as if every city had fallen to the enemy. For everywhere there was utter chaos, and nothing was ever the same again: in the confusion that followed, the laws and the orderly structure of the State were turned upside down.

To begin with, the partisans changed the style of their hair to a quite novel fashion, having it cut very differently from the other Romans. They did not touch moustache or beard at all, but were always anxious to let them grow as long as possible, like the Persians. But the hair on the front of the head they cut right back to the temples, allowing the growth behind to hang down to its full length in a disorderly mass, like the Massagetae. That is why they sometimes called this the Hunnish style. Then as regards dress, they all thought it necessary to be luxuriously turned out, donning attire too ostentatious for their particular station. For they were in a position to obtain such garments at other people's expense. The part of the tunic covering their arms was drawn in very tight at the wrists, while from there to the shoulders it spread out to an enormous width. Whenever they waved their arms as they shouted in the theatre or the hippodrome and encouraged their favourites in the usual way, up in the air went this part of their tunics, giving silly people the notion that their bodies were so splendidly sturdy that they had to be covered with garments of this kind: they did not realize that the transparency and emptiness of their attire rather served to show up their miserable physique. Their capes and breeches too, and in most cases their shoes, were classed as Hunnish in name and fashion.

At first the great majority carried weapons at night quite openly, while in the day time they concealed short two-edged swords along their thighs under their cloaks. They used to collect in gangs at nightfall and rob members of the upper class in the whole forum or in narrow lanes, despoiling any they met of cloaks, belts, gold brooches, and anything else they had with them. Some they thought it better to murder as well as rob, since dead men told no tales. These outrages caused universal indignation, especially in those Blues who were not militant partisans, since they suffered as badly as the rest. Consequently from then on most people wore belts and brooches of bronze, and cloaks of much poorer quality than their station warranted, for fear that their love of the beautiful would cost them their lives; and even before sunset they hurried back home and got under cover. As this shocking state of affairs continued and no notice was taken of the offenders by the authorities in charge of the city, the audacity of these men increased by leaps and bounds. For when nothing is done to discourage wrongdoing there is of course no limit to its growth: even when punishment does follow offences it does not often put an end to them altogether: it is natural for most people to turn easily to wrongdoing.

That is how things went with the Blues. Of their opponents some came over to their faction through a desire to join in their criminal activities without paying any penalty, others took to flight and slipped away to other countries; many who were caught in the city were put out of the way by their opponents or executed by the authorities. Many other young men poured into this organization: they had never before shown any interest in such things, but ambition for power and unrestrained licence attracted them to it. For there is not one revolting crime known to men which was not at that time committed and left unpunished. They began by destroying the partisans of the opposite faction, then went on to murder those who had given them no excuse whatever. Many also won them with bribes, then indicated their own enemies; these the partisans got rid of at once, labelling them Greens though they knew nothing at all about them. All this went on no longer in darkness or out of sight, but at any moment of the day and in every part of the city, and the most eminent citizens as often as not were eyewitnesses of what was happening. There was no need to keep the crimes concealed, since the criminals were not troubled by any fear of punishment; in fact they were actually moved by a spirit of rivalry, so that they organized displays of brawn and toughness to show that with a single blow they could kill anyone they met unarmed, and no one now could expect to live much longer amid the dangers that daily threatened him. Constant fear made everyone suspect that death was just round the corner: no place seemed safe, no time could guarantee security, since even in the most revered churches

and at public festivals people were being senselessly murdered, and confidence in kith and kin was a thing of the past.
For many perished through the machinations of their nearest
relatives.

No inquiry, however, was held into the crimes committed: the blow invariably fell without warning, and the
fallen had no one to avenge them. No law or contract
retained any force on the secure basis of established order,
but everything turned to growing violence and confusion,
and the government was indistinguishable from a tyranny;
not however a stable tyranny, but one that changed every
day and was for ever starting afresh. The decisions of the
magistrates suggested the paralysis of fear; their minds
were dominated by dread of a single man; while juries, when
settling questions in dispute, based their verdicts, not on
their notions of what was just and lawful, but on the relations, hostile or friendly, which each of the disputants had
with the partisans. For any juror who disregarded their
injunctions would pay the penalty with his life.

Many creditors were under irresistible pressure to return
the written agreements to their debtors without recovering
a penny of the debt, and many people to their chagrin had
to free their domestic servants; and it is said that a number of
women were forced by their own slaves to yield to many
suggestions most repugnant to them. And by now the sons
of men in high positions, after associating with these young
criminals, compelled their fathers to do a number of things
they were most reluctant to do, and particularly to hand
over their money to them. Many unwilling boys, with the
full knowledge of their fathers, were forced into immoral
relations with the partisans; and women who were happily

married suffered the same humiliation. It is said that one woman, very elegantly attired, was sailing with her husband to one of the suburbs on the mainland opposite; and during this crossing the partisans intercepted them, tore the lady from her husband's arms, and carried her to their own boat. Before going on board with the young men she whispered encouragement to her husband and told him to have no fear on her account: she would never submit to physical outrage. Then, while her husband was still watching her through his tears, she jumped overboard, and from that moment was never seen again.

Such were the acts of violence of which at that period the partisans in Byzantium were guilty. But these things caused less misery to the victims than the wrongs which the community suffered at Justinian's hands, because those whom miscreants have injured the most cruelly are relieved of most of the misery resulting from a disordered society by the constant expectation that the laws and the government will punish the offenders. For when people are confident of the future they find their present troubles more tolerable and easier to bear; but when they are subjected to violence by the State authorities they are naturally more distressed by the wrongs they have suffered, and fall into utter despair through the hopelessness of expecting justice. Justinian betrayed his subjects not only because he absolutely refused to uphold the victims of wrong, but because he was perfectly prepared to set himself up as the recognized champion of the partisans; for he lavished great sums of money on these young men and kept many of them in his entourage, actually promoting some to magistracies and other official positions.

Such then was the state of affairs in Byzantium and everywhere else. For like any other disease the infection that
began in the capital rapidly spread all over the Roman
Empire. The Emperor took no notice at all of what was
going on, since he was a man incapable of perception,
although he was invariably an eyewitness of all that happened in the hippodromes. For he was extremely simple,
with no more sense than a donkey, ready to follow anyone
who pulls the rein, waving its ears all the time.

While Justinian behaved in this way he was making a mess
of everything else. He had no sooner seized upon his uncle's
authority than he began to squander public money in the
most reckless manner and with the greatest satisfaction, now
that he had got it in his hands. From time to time he came in
contact with some of the Huns, and showered money on
them 'for services to the State'. The inevitable result was
that Roman territory was exposed to constant incursions.
For after tasting the wealth of the Romans these barbarians
could never again keep away from the road to the capital.
Again, he did not hesitate to throw vast sums into erecting
buildings along the sea-front in the hope of checking the
constant surge of the waves. He pushed forward from the
shore by heaping up stones, in his determination to defeat
the onrush of the water, and in his efforts to rival, as it were,
the strength of the sea by the power of wealth.

He gathered into his own hands the private property of
all the Romans in every land, either accusing them of some
crime they had never committed, or coaxing them into the
belief that they had made him a free gift. Many who had
been convicted of murders and other capital crimes made
over to him their entire property, and so escaped without

paying the penalty of their offences. Others, who were perhaps laying claim without any justification to lands belonging
to their neighbours, found it impossible to win judgement against their opponents because they had no legal
case; so they actually made the Emperor a present of the
property in dispute and got clear of the whole business: they
themselves by generosity that cost nothing secured an introduction to His Majesty, and by the most unlawful means
managed to get the better of their opponents.

At this point, I think, it would be well to describe Justinian's personal appearance. In build he was neither tall nor
unusually short, but of normal height; not at all skinny but
rather plump, with a round face that was not unattractive:
it retained its healthy colour even after a two-day fast. To
describe his general appearance in a word, he bore a strong
resemblance to Domitian, Vespasian's son, whose monstrous
behaviour left such a mark upon the Romans that even when
they had carved up his whole body they did not feel that
they had exhausted their indignation against him: the Senate
passed a decree that not even the name of this emperor
should remain in inscriptions, nor any statue or portrait of
him be preserved. Certainly from the inscriptions everywhere in Rome, and wherever else his name had been in-
scribed, it was chiselled out, as can still be seen, leaving all
the rest intact; and nowhere in the Roman Empire is there a
single·likeness of him except for a solitary bronze statue,
which survived in the following way.

Domitian's consort was a woman of good birth, and
highly respected, who had herself never done the least
wrong to any man alive, or approved a single one of her

husband's actions. So she was very highly esteemed, and the Senate at this time sent for her and invited her to ask for anything she liked. She made only one request – that she might take Domitian's body and bury it, and set up a bronze statue of him in a place of her own choosing. The Senate agreed to this; and the widow, wishing to leave to later generations a monument to the inhumanity of those who had carved up her husband, devised the following plan. Having collected Domitian's flesh, she put the pieces together carefully and fitted them to each other; then she stitched the whole body together and showed it to the sculptors, asking them to make a bronze statue portraying the tragic end of the dead man. The artists produced the statue without loss of time; and the widow took it and erected it in the street that leads up to the Capitol, on the right-hand side as you go there from the Forum: it showed the appearance and the tragic end of Domitian, and does so to this day. It seems probable that Justinian's general build, his actual expression, and all the characteristic details of his visage are clearly portrayed in this statue.[1]

Such then was his outward appearance; his character was beyond my powers of accurate description. For he was both prone to evil-doing and easily led astray – both knave and fool, to use a common phrase: he never spoke the truth

1. This extraordinary story, already current before Procopius's time, seems to have been invented to account for the strange appearance of the statue. It was probably not Domitian's corpse but his statue that had been pieced together, it having been smashed like the others by order of the Senate. As for the devoted widow, Domitia, there is little doubt that she had a hand in her husband's murder.

himself to those he happened to be with, but in everything that he said or did there was always a dishonest purpose; yet to anyone who wanted to deceive him he was easy meat. He was by nature an extraordinary mixture of folly and wickedness inseparably blended. This perhaps was an instance of what one of the Peripatetic philosophers suggested many years ago – that exactly opposite qualities may on occasions be combined in a man's nature just as in the blending of colours. However, I must limit my description to facts of which I have been able to make sure.

Well, then, this emperor was dissembling, crafty, hypocritical, secretive by temperament, two-faced; a clever fellow with a marvellous ability to conceal his real opinion, and able to shed tears, not from any joy or sorrow, but employing them artfully when required in accordance with the immediate need, lying all the time; not carelessly, however, but confirming his undertakings both with his signature and with the most fearsome oaths, even when dealing with his own subjects. But he promptly disregarded both agreements and solemn pledges, like the most contemptible slaves, who by fear of the tortures hanging over them are driven to confess misdeeds they have denied on oath. A treacherous friend and an inexorable enemy, he was passionately devoted to murder and plunder; quarrelsome and subversive in the extreme; easily led astray into evil ways but refusing every suggestion that he should follow the right path; quick to devise vile schemes and to carry them out; and with an instinctive aversion to the mere mention of anything good.

How could anyone find words to describe Justinian's character? These vices and many yet greater he clearly possessed to an inhuman degree: it seemed as if nature had removed every tendency to evil from the rest of mankind and deposited it in the soul of this man. In addition to everything else he was far too ready to listen to false accusations, and quick to inflict punishment. For he never ferreted out the facts before passing judgement, but on hearing the accusations immediately had his verdict announced. Without hesitation he issued orders for the seizure of towns, the burning of cities, and the enslavement of entire nations, for no reason at all. So that if one chose to add up all the calamities which have befallen the Romans from the beginning and to weigh them against those for which Justinian was responsible, I feel sure that he would find that a greater slaughter of human beings was brought about by this one man than took place in all the preceding centuries. As for other people's money, he seized it by stealth without the slightest hesitation; for he did not even think it necessary to put forward any excuse or pretence of justification before taking possession of things to which he had no claim. Yet when he had secured the money he was quite prepared to show his contempt for it by reckless prodigality, or to throw it to potential enemies without the slightest need. In short, he kept no money himself and allowed no one else in the world to keep any, as if he were not overcome by avarice but held fast by envy of those who had acquired money. Thus he cheerfully banished wealth from Roman soil and became the creator of nation-wide poverty.

The features of Justinian's character, then, as far as I am in a position to state them, were roughly as suggested above.

He married a wife, whose origin and upbringing I must

now explain, and how after becoming his consort she destroyed the Roman State root and branch.

In Byzantium there was a man called Acacius, a keeper of the circus animals, belonging to the Green faction and entitled the Bearward. This man died of sickness while Anastasius occupied the imperial throne, leaving three daughters, Comito, Theodora, and Anastasia, of whom the eldest had not yet completed her seventh year. The widow married again, hoping that her new husband would from then on share with her the management of her house and the care of the animals. But the Greens' Dancing-master, a man called Asterius, was offered a bribe to remove these two from their office, in which he installed his Paymaster without any difficulty, for the Dancing-masters were allowed to arrange such matters just as they chose. But when the wife saw the whole populace congregated in the circus, she put wreaths on the heads of the little girls and in both their hands, and made them sit down as suppliants. The Greens refused absolutely to admit the supplication; but the Blues gave them a similar office, as their Bearward too had died.

When the children were old enough, they were at once put on the stage there by their mother, as their appearance was very attractive; not all at the same time, however, but as each one seemed to her to be mature enough for this profession. The eldest one, Comito, was already one of the most popular harlots of the day. Theodora, who came next, clad in a little tunic with long sleeves, the usual dress of a slave girl, used to assist her in various ways, following her about and invariably carrying on her shoulders the bench on which her sister habitually sat at public meetings. For the time being Theodora was still too undeveloped to be capable of sharing a man's bed or having intercourse like a woman; but she acted as a sort of male prostitute to satisfy customers of the lowest type, and slaves at that, who when accompanying their owners to the theatre seized their opportunity to divert themselves in this revolting manner; and for some considerable time she remained in a brothel, given up to this unnatural bodily commerce. But as soon as she was old enough and fully developed, she joined the women on the stage and promptly became a courtesan, of the type our ancestors called 'the dregs of the army'. For she was not a flautist or harpist; she was not even qualified to join the corps of dancers; but she merely sold her attractions to anyone who came along, putting her whole body at his disposal.

Later she joined the actors in all the business of the theatre and played a regular part in their stage performances, making herself the butt of their ribald buffoonery. She was extremely clever and had a biting wit, and quickly became popular as a result. There was not a particle of modesty in the little hussy, and no one ever saw her taken aback: she complied with the most outrageous demands without the slightest hesitation, and she was the sort of girl who if somebody walloped her or boxed her ears would make a jest of it and roar with laughter; and she would throw off her clothes and exhibit naked to all and sundry those regions, both in front and behind, which the rules of decency require to be kept veiled and hidden from masculine eyes.

She used to tease her lovers by keeping them waiting, and by constantly playing about with novel methods of intercourse she could always bring the lascivious to her feet; so far from waiting to be invited by anyone she encountered,

she herself by cracking dirty jokes and wiggling her hips
suggestively would invite all who came her way, especially
if they were still in their teens. Never was anyone so completely given up to unlimited self-indulgence. Often she
would go to a bring-your-own-food dinner-party with ten
young men or more, all at the peak of their physical powers
and with fornication as their chief object in life, and would
lie with all her fellow-diners in turn the whole night long:
when she had reduced them all to a state of exhaustion she
would go to their menials, as many as thirty on occasions,
and copulate with every one of them; but not even so could
she satisfy her lust.

One night she went into the house of a distinguished
citizen during the drinking, and, it is said, before the eyes
of all the guests she stood up on the end of the couch near
their feet, pulled up her dress in the most disgusting manner
as she stood there, and brazenly displayed her lasciviousness.
And though she brought three openings into service, she
often found fault with Nature, grumbling because Nature
had not made the openings in her nipples wider than is
normal, so that she could devise another variety of intercourse in that region. Naturally she was frequently pregnant,
but by using pretty well all the tricks of the trade she was
able to induce immediate abortion.

Often in the theatre, too, in full view of all the people she
would throw off her clothes and stand naked in their midst,
having only a girdle about her private parts and her groins –
not, however, because she was ashamed to expose these also
to the public, but because no one is allowed to appear there
absolutely naked: a girdle round the groins is compulsory.
With this minimum covering she would spread herself out

and lie face upwards on the floor. Servants on whom this task had been imposed would sprinkle barley grains over her private parts, and geese trained for the purpose used to pick them off one by one with their bills and swallow them. Theodora, so far from blushing when she stood up again, actually seemed to be proud of this performance. For she was not only shameless herself, but did more than anyone else to encourage shamelessness.

Many times she threw off her clothes and stood in the middle of the actors on the stage, leaning over backwards or pushing out her behind to invite both those who had already enjoyed her and those who had not been intimate as yet, parading her own special brand of gymnastics. With such lasciviousness did she misuse her own body that she appeared to have her private parts not like other women in the place intended by nature, but in her face! And again, those who were intimate with her showed by so doing that they were not having intercourse in accordance with the laws of nature; and every person of any decency who happened to meet her in the forum would swing round and beat a hasty retreat, for fear he might come in contact with any of the hussy's garments and so appear tainted with this pollution. For to those who saw her, especially in the early hours of the day, she was a bird of ill omen. As for her fellow-actresses, she habitually and constantly stormed at them like a fury; for she was malicious in the extreme.

Later she accompanied Hecebolus, a Tyrian who had taken over the government of Pentapolis,[1] in order to serve him in the most revolting capacity, but she got into bad odour with him and was shot out without more ado; as a

1. A group of five cities in Libya.

result she found herself without even the necessities of life, which from then on she provided in her customary fashion by making her body the tool of her lawless trade. First she came to Alexandria; then after making a tour round the whole East she returned to Byzantium, in every city following an occupation which a man had better not name, I think, if he hopes ever to enjoy the favour of God. It was as if the unseen powers could not allow any spot on earth to be unaware of Theodora's depravity.

Such, then, was the birth and upbringing of this woman, the subject of common talk among women of the streets and among people of every kind. But when she arrived back in Byzantium Justinian conceived an overpowering passion for her. At first he consorted with her only as a mistress, though he did promote her to Patrician rank. This at once enabled Theodora to possess herself of immense influence and of very considerable wealth. For as so often happens to men consumed with passion, it seemed in Justinian's eyes the most delightful thing in the world to lavish all his favours and all his wealth upon the object of his passion. And the whole State became fuel for this passion. With Theodora to help him he impoverished the people far more than before, not only in the capital but in every part of the Empire. As both had long been supporters of the Blue Faction, they gave the members of this faction immense powers over State affairs. It was a very long time before the evil was mitigated to any great extent. It happened in this way.

Justinian suffered from a prolonged illness, which brought him into such extreme danger that he was even reported to be dead. All the time the factionists were misbehaving in the ways already described, and one Hypatius, a man of some distinction, was murdered by them in full daylight in the Church of Sophia. When this crime had been committed, the disorders it provoked were reported to the Emperor; and all those about him, seizing the opportunity provided by Justinian's absence from public affairs, did everything they could to emphasize the gravity of what had occurred, giving him a complete list of all the happenings from beginning to end. At that the Emperor instructed the Prefect of the City to bring all the offenders to justice. This official was named Theodotus, but was generally referred to as the Pumpkin. He made a thorough examination of all concerned, and was able to arrest many of the perpetrators and sentence them to execution according to the law, though many of them slipped through his fingers and escaped. At a later date they were to share the ruin of the Empire.[1]

Contrary to expectation the Emperor suddenly recovered, and actually took steps to get rid of Theodotus as a poisoner and magician. But as he could invent no possible pretext to justify his destroying him, he subjected some of the man's friends to the most horrible torments, and drove them to make accusations against him that were without foundation. When all others kept out of his way and remained discreetly silent about their distress at his machinations against Theodotus, Proclus alone, who held the quaestorship, as it was called, openly asserted that the accused man was innocent of the charge and had done nothing to deserve death. In consequence Theodotus, on the suggestion of the Emperor, conveyed himself away to Jerusalem. But it came to his knowledge that men had arrived there who were bent on

1. The Greek is corrupt and cannot be emended with certainty.

getting rid of him; so ever after that he remained hidden in the church, and never emerged till the day of his death.

Of Theodotus there is no more to be said. But the factionists from that time on became the most prudent people in the world. They no longer ventured to misbehave in such shocking ways, though they had every opportunity to follow their career of lawlessness with even greater impunity. Here is evidence enough: when a few of them later showed similar audacity, they suffered no penalty whatsoever. For those authorized to inflict punishment invariably provided the perpetrators of crimes with every opportunity to evade it, encouraging them by this connivance to trample on the laws.

As long as the Empress was still alive, it was quite impossible for Justinian to make Theodora his lawful wife. On this one point the Empress opposed him, though she objected to none of his other actions. For the old lady abhorred anything improper, though she was completely without culture and was of barbarian origin, as stated earlier. She was quite incapable of making any mark, and remained utterly ignorant of State affairs; in fact she dropped her real name, which she felt to be ridiculous, before entering the Palace, and assumed the name Euphemia. But some time later it happened that the Empress died. Justin was in his dotage and quite senile, so that he became the laughing-stock of his subjects, treated by everyone with complete contempt because of his ignorance of what was happening, and left out of account; Justinian on the other hand was greatly feared and assiduously courted, for he stirred up trouble all the time, producing universal turmoil and confusion. This was the moment he chose for arranging his engagement to Theodora. But as it was impossible for a man who had reached the rank of senator to make a courtesan his wife, such a thing being prohibited from the beginning by the most venerable laws, he forced the Emperor to abrogate the laws by establishing a new one. From that moment he lived with Theodora as his legal spouse, thereby enabling everyone else to get engaged to a courtesan. Then by one bold stroke he seized upon the imperial office, fabricating an excuse to disguise the high-handedness of his action. He was proclaimed Emperor of the Romans, in conjunction with his uncle, by all the aristocracy, whom overpowering fear compelled to vote in this way. Imperial authority was assumed by Justinian and Theodora three days before the Feast,[1] a time when one is not allowed to greet any of one's friends or to wish him good day. A few days later Justin died from natural causes, after reigning nine years,[2] and Justinian in conjunction with Theodora became sole monarch.

So it came about that Theodora born, brought up, and educated as described above, despite all obstacles mounted the imperial throne. It never even occurred to her husband that his conduct was shocking, though he was in a position to take his pick of the Roman Empire and select for his bride the most nobly born woman in the world, who had enjoyed the most exclusive upbringing, and was thoroughly acquainted with the claims of modesty, and had lived in an atmosphere of chastity, and in addition was superbly beautiful and still a virgin – or, as they say, firm-breasted. No: he must needs make the common bane of all mankind his very own, oblivious of all the facts recorded in these pages, and consort with a woman double-dyed with every kind of

1. Easter.   2. A.D. 518 to 527.

horrible pollution, and guilty over and over again of infanticide by wilful abortion.

Not one thing more need be mentioned, I think, regarding the character of this man: this marriage would be quite enough to reveal only too clearly all his moral sickness; it was both interpreter, witness, and chronicler of the course he followed. For when a man cares nothing for the infamy of his actions, and does not hesitate to be known to all and sundry as a revolting character, no path of lawlessness is closed to him, but armed with the shamelessness visible at every moment in his face, he advances cheerfully and without any misgivings to the most loathsome deeds.

Sad to say, not even one member of the Senate, seeing the State saddling itself with this disgrace, saw fit to protest and to oppose such proceedings, though they would all have to fall down before her as if she were a goddess. There was not even one priest who showed any disgust, and that when they would be obliged to address her as 'Mistress'. And the people who had previously watched her performances in the theatre instantly thought fit to be in fact and name her grovelling slaves. Nor did one soldier resent being called on to face danger on the battlefield for Theodora's benefit; nor did any other living person oppose her. All of them, I imagine, were subdued by the thought that this was the fate assigned to them, and accordingly lifted no finger to prevent this revolting state of affairs, as though Fortune had given a demonstration of her power; for as she controls all human affairs it is a matter of complete indifference to her that what is done shall be justifiable, or that men shall feel that there was reason behind what has happened already. Suddenly by an unreasoning display of power she uplifts to a lofty eminence a man who seems to have been entangled hitherto in one difficulty after another; she offers no resistance to anything on earth that he takes in hand, and all things conspire to hurry him along to whatever goal she has seen fit to choose for him, while all mankind stand back without hesitation and make way for Fortune as she goes ahead. But we must leave it to God to decide how these things shall be and how they shall be spoken of.

As for Theodora, she had an attractive face and a good figure, but was short and pallid, though not in an extreme degree, for there was just a trace of colour. Her glance was invariably fierce and intensely hard. If I were to attempt a detailed account of her life upon the stage, I could go on for the rest of time; but the few incidents picked out for inclusion in the preceding paragraphs should be enough to give a complete picture of this woman's character, for the enlightenment of those yet to come.

Now we must sketch the outlines of what she and her husband did in unison, for neither did anything apart from the other to the end of their joint lives. For a long time it was universally believed that they were exact opposites in their ideas and interests; but later it was recognized that this false impression had been deliberately fostered to make sure that their subjects did not put their own differences aside and rebel against them, but were all divided in their feelings about them. They began by creating a division between the Christians; and by pretending to take opposite sides in religious disputes they split the whole body in two, as will shortly be made clear.[1] Then they kept the factions at loggerheads. The Empress made out that she was throwing her full

1. See page 177.

weight behind the Blues, and by extending to them full authority to assail the opposite faction she made it possible for them to disregard all restrictions and perform outrageous deeds of criminal violence. Her husband replied by behaving as if he were boiling over with bottled-up resentment, but was unable to stand up to his wife overtly, and often they confounded the character of their authority and went opposite ways. He, for instance, was determined to punish the Blues as criminal offenders, while she in a synthetic rage would complain bitterly that she had 'yielded to her husband under protest'. And yet the Blue partisans, as I said before, seemed to be the most orderly; for they were satisfied that it was quite unjustifiable to go to the limit in doing violence to one's neighbours. Again, in the bitter animosities aroused by lawsuits each of the two appeared to be backing one of the litigants, and it was so arranged that victory should go to the one who championed the unjust cause,[1] and that in this way the two of them should purloin most of the wealth of both contestants.

Finally, many were included in this emperor's list of intimate friends and raised to positions which enabled them to violate the laws and commit offences against the State to their heart's content; but as soon as it was evident that they had made their pile, they promptly came into collision with Theodora and found themselves in her bad books. At first Justinian was perfectly prepared to declare himself their enthusiastic supporter, but later on his sympathy for the poor fellows would dry up, and his zeal on their behalf would become very uncertain. That would be the signal for his partner to damage them beyond recovery while he,

1. A reminiscence of Aristophanes' *Clouds*.

shutting his eyes tight to what was going on, opened his arms to receive their entire possessions, thus shamelessly acquired. In practising these tricks they invariably collaborated, though in public they acted as if they were at daggers drawn; thus they succeeded in dividing their subjects, and in so strengthening their hold that it could never be shaken off.

CHAPTER 3

Justinian's Misgovernment

WHEN Justinian ascended the throne it took him a very little while to bring everything into confusion. Things hitherto forbidden by law were one by one brought into public life, while established customs were swept away wholesale, as if he had been invested with the forms of majesty on condition that he would change all things to new forms. Long established offices were abolished, and new ones set up to run the nation's business; the laws of the land and the organization of the army were treated in the same way, not because justice required it or the general interest urged him to it, but merely that everything might have a new look and might be associated with his name. If there was anything which he was not in a position to transform then and there, even so he would at least attach his own name to it.

Of the forcible seizure of property and the murder of his subjects he could never have enough: when he had looted innumerable houses of wealthy people he was constantly on the look-out for others, immediately squandering on one foreign tribe or another, or on crazy building schemes, all that he had amassed by his earlier looting. And when he had without any excuse got rid of thousands and thousands of people, or so it would seem, he promptly devised schemes for doing the same to others more numerous still.

At that time the Romans were at peace with all other nations; so not knowing how to satisfy his lust for blood Justinian kept flinging all the foreign nations at each other's throats; and sending for the chieftains of the Huns, though he had no reason at all, with senseless prodigality he flung vast sums into their laps, making out, if you please, that these were pledges of friendship. This he was stated to have done even when Justin was on the throne. They for their part, having received this windfall, used to send some of their brother-chieftains at the head of their men, urging them to make sudden raids into the Emperor's territory, so that they too might be in a position to exact a price for peace from the man who for no reason at all was prepared to pay for it. These chiefs at once began the enslavement of the Roman Empire, and all the time they were in the Emperor's pay. Their example was immediately followed by others, who joined in the pillaging of the unfortunate Romans, and on top of the pillage received as a reward for their inroads the extravagant largesse of the Emperor. Thus, in short, from year's end to year's end they all took turns to plunder and pillage everything within their reach. For these native races have many groups of chieftains, and the war was passed from one group to another in rotation as a result of Justinian's inexcusable prodigality; it could never come to an end, but went on circling round itself month after month, year after year. And so no single patch of ground, mountain, cave, or anything else on Roman soil, escaped being pillaged at this time, and many places were actually overrun five times or more. These calamities, however, and all those suffered at the hands of Medes, Saracens, Slavs, Antae, and other foreign nations, have been recounted in my earlier volumes; but as I said in the first paragraph of the present volume, it is essential that I should make clear now where the responsibility lay for all that happened.

To Chosroes Justinian handed over vast sums in gold to secure peace; then with inexcusable disregard of anyone else's opinion he made himself responsible for the breaking of the truce by his determination to effect a partnership with Alamundarus and his Huns, who were in alliance with the Persians, as in my chapter on the subject[1] was revealed plainly enough, I think. While he was stirring up the faction-fights and wars which brought such miseries on the Romans, and fanning the blaze with this one object only, that by all possible means the earth should be filled with human blood and that still more plunder should fall into his hands, he devised yet another horrible massacre of his subjects. It happened in this way.

Throughout the Roman Empire there are many unorthodox beliefs generally known as heresies – Montanism, Sabbatarianism, and numerous others which continually lead men into doctrinal error. All the adherents of these were ordered to renounce their former beliefs under threat of many penalties for disobedience, above all the withdrawal of the right to bequeath their possessions to their children or relations. The churches of these heretics, as they are called, especially those who professed the doctrine of Arius, possessed unheard-of riches. Neither the whole Senate nor any other very large body in the Roman State could compete in wealth with these churches. They possessed treasures of gold and silver, and ornaments covered with precious stones, beyond description and beyond counting, houses and villages in great numbers, and many acres of land in all quarters of the world, and every other kind of wealth that exists and is named anywhere on earth, since none of the long line of

1. Book II, 1.

emperors had ever interfered with them. A great number of people, even though they held orthodox beliefs, depended upon them at all times for their livelihood, justifying themselves on the ground that they were merely following their regular occupations. So by first of all confiscating the property of these churches the Emperor Justinian suddenly robbed them of all they possessed. The result was that from that moment most of the men were deprived of their only means of support.

An army of officials was at once sent out in all directions to force everyone they met to renounce his ancestral beliefs. In the eyes of country people such a suggestion was blasphemous; so they resolved one and all to stand their ground against the men who made this demand. Many in consequence perished at the hands of the soldiers; many even put an end to their own lives, being foolish enough to think this the godliest course; and the great majority abandoned the land of their birth and went into banishment. But the Montanists, who were established in Phrygia, shut themselves up in their own churches and at once set these buildings on fire, perishing with them for no reason at all. The result was that the whole Roman Empire was one great scene of slaughter and banishment.

A similar law being next passed in respect of the Samaritans, tumultuous disorders descended upon Palestine. All who lived in my own Caesarea and the other cities, thinking it silly to endure any sort of distress for the sake of a nonsensical dogma, discarded their old name and called themselves Christians, managing by this pretence to shake off the danger threatened by the law. Those among them who were at all prudent and reasonable were quite agreeable to remaining loyal to their new faith; but the majority, apparently feeling indignant that in defiance of their wishes they were being compelled by this law to abandon the beliefs they had inherited, very soon defected to the Manichees and 'Polytheists'. But the peasants at a mass meeting resolved as one man to take up arms against the Emperor, putting forward as the emperor of their own choice a bandit named Julian, son of Savarus. They joined battle with the soldiers and held out for some time, but in the end they lost the fight and were cut to pieces, together with their leader. It is said that a hundred thousand men lost their lives in this engagement, and the most fertile land in the world was left with no one to till it. For the owners of these acres, Christians one and all, this business had disastrous consequences; for though the land was yielding them no profit at all, they were compelled to pay to the Emperor in perpetuity annual taxes on a crippling scale, since these demands were pressed relentlessly.

Next he turned the persecution against the 'Greeks',[1] torturing their bodies and looting their property. Many of these decided to assume for appearance' sake the name of Christian in order to avert the immediate threat; but it was not long before they were for the most part caught at their libations and sacrifices and other unholy rites. What was done in respect of the Christians I shall explain in a later volume.[2]

After that he passed a law forbidding offences against boys, not inquiring closely into those committed after the passing of the law, but seeking out men who had succumbed

1. Adherents of the old paganism.
2. See note on page 41.

to this moral sickness some time in the past. The prosecution of these offenders was conducted in the most irregular fashion, since the penalty was imposed even where there was no accuser, and the word of a single man or boy, even if he happened to be a slave forced to give evidence most unwillingly against his owner, was accepted as final proof. Men convicted in this way were castrated and exposed to public ribaldry. At first, however, not everyone was treated in this shocking manner, but only those who were thought to be either Greens or exceptionally well off, or who happened to have come up against the rulers in some other way.

Again, they were bitterly hostile to the astrologers. Accordingly the official appointed to deal with burglaries made a point of ill-treating them simply because they were astrologers, flogging the backs of many of them and setting them on camels to be shown to jeering crowds all over the city, though they were old men and respectable in every way. Yet he had nothing against them except that they wished to be authorities on the stars in such a place as this. As a result, great numbers of people were constantly slipping away, not only to foreign countries but also to distant regions in Roman occupation, and in every district and city there were always masses of new faces to be seen. For to avoid being caught every man was glad to exchange his homeland for another country, as if his own had fallen into enemy hands.

So it was that the possessions of those considered well-to-do in Byzantium and every other city (next after members of the Senate) were plundered, in the way described, by Justinian and Theodora, and remained in their hands. How they managed to rob the senators too of all their property I will now explain.

There was in Byzantium a man called Zeno, grandson of the Anthemius who had earlier become Emperor of the West. To serve their own ends they appointed this man Governor of Egypt and dispatched him there. But Zeno packed all his most valuable effects on board ship and got ready to sail; for he had an immeasurable weight of silver, and vessels of solid gold embellished with pearls and emeralds, and with other stones equally precious. Their Majesties then bribed some of those whose loyalty he trusted completely to remove the precious cargo with all speed and drop firebrands into the hold of the ship, after which they were to inform Zeno that the blaze had broken out spontaneously in the vessel and that the entire cargo had been lost. Not long after, as it happened, Zeno died very suddenly, and the two of them promptly took over his estate as his lawful heirs; for they produced a will of sorts, which it was openly rumoured was not of his making.

By similar methods they made themselves heirs of Tatian, Demosthenes, and Hilara, who in rank and all other respects were leading members of the Roman Senate. The property of certain others they acquired by forging not wills but letters. That was how they became heirs of Dionysius, who lived in Lebanon, and of John, the son of Basilius. John had been quite the most distinguished man in all Edessa, but Belisarius had handed him over willy-nilly as a hostage to the Persians, as recounted by me in an earlier volume.[1] Chosroes finally refused to let this man go, accusing the

1. Book II.

Romans of breaking all the agreements under which Belisarius had handed him over; however, he was prepared to
sell him as being now a prisoner of war. John's grandmother,
who was still alive, furnished the ransom, amounting to
two thousand pounds' weight of silver,[1] in the full expectation of redeeming her grandson. But when this ransom had
arrived in Daras the Emperor got to know of it and forbade
the completion of the transaction – in order, he said, that
Roman wealth might not be transferred to a foreign power.
Shortly after this John fell sick and departed this life;
whereupon the chief administrator of the city concocted a
letter of sorts which he said John had recently written to
him as a friend, to inform him that he desired his whole
estate to go to the Emperor. It would be beyond me to list
the names of all the others whose heirs they contrived to
become.

Until the 'Nika' insurrection took place,[2] they were
content to annex the estates of the well-to-do one at a time;
but after it took place, as I related in an earlier volume,[3]
from then on they confiscated at a single stroke the possessions of nearly all the senators. On all movable property
and on the most attractive landed estates they laid their
hands just as they fancied; but they set aside properties liable
to oppressive and crushing taxation, and with sham generosity *sold* them to their previous owners! These in consequence were throttled by the tax-collectors and reduced
to penury by the never-ending interest on their debts,

1. Now worth £11,200
2. In A.D. 532 the Blue and Green factions united in a desperate
revolt against Justinian.
3. Book I.

dragging out a miserable existence that was no more than a lingering death.

In view of all this I, like most of my contemporaries, never once felt that these two were human beings: they were a pair of blood-thirsty demons and what the poets[1] call 'plaguers of mortal men'. For they plotted together to find the easiest and swiftest means of destroying all races of men and all their works, assumed human shape, became man-demons, and in this way convulsed the whole world. Proof of this could be found in many things, but especially in the power manifested in their doings. For the actions of demons are unmistakably different from those of human beings. In the long course of time there have doubtless been many men who by chance or by nature have inspired the utmost fear, and by their unaided efforts have ruined cities or countries or whatever it might be; but to bring destruction on all mankind and calamities on the whole world has been beyond the power of any but these two, who were, it is true, aided in their endeavours by chance, which collaborated in the ruin of mankind; for earthquakes, pestilences, and rivers that burst their banks brought wide-spread destruction at this time, as I shall explain shortly. Thus it was not by human but by some very different power that they wrought such havoc.

It is said that Justinian's own mother told some of her close friends that he was not the son of her husband Sabbatius or of any man at all. For when she was about to conceive she was visited by a demon, who was invisible but gave her a distinct impression that he was really there with her like a

1. Homer and Aeschylus.

man in bodily contact with a woman. Then he vanished like a dream.

Some of those who were in the Emperor's company late at night, conversing with him (evidently in the Palace) – men of the highest possible character – thought that they saw a strange demonic form in his place. One of them declared that he more than once rose suddenly from the imperial throne and walked round and round the room; for he was not in the habit of remaining seated for long. And Justinian's head would momentarily disappear, while the rest of his body seemed to continue making these long circuits. The watcher himself, thinking that something had gone seriously wrong with his eyesight, stood for a long time distressed and quite at a loss. But later the head returned to the body, and he thought that what a moment before had been lacking was, contrary to expectation, filling out again. A second man said that he stood by the Emperor's side as he sat, and saw his face suddenly transformed to a shapeless lump of flesh: neither eyebrows nor eyes were in their normal position, and it showed no other distinguishing feature at all; gradually, however, he saw the face return to its usual shape. I did not myself witness the events I am describing, but I heard about them from men who insist that they saw them at the time.

It is also related that a certain monk highly favoured by God was persuaded by those who lived with him in the desert to set out for Byzantium in order to speak on behalf of their nearest neighbours, who were suffering violence and injustice beyond bearing. On his arrival there he was at once admitted to the Emperor's presence; but when he was on the point of entering the audience chamber and had put

one foot inside the door, he suddenly drew it back and
retreated. The eunuch who was escorting him and others
who were present urged and encouraged him to go on; but
he gave no answer, and as if he had suddenly gone crazy
he dashed away back to the apartment where he was lodging.
When those who accompanied him asked him to explain
this strange behaviour, we understand that he said straight
out that he had seen the King of the Demons in the Palace,
sitting on the throne, and he was not prepared to meet him
or to ask any favour of him.

After all, how could this man be other than a wicked
demon, when he never satisfied his natural appetite for
drink, food, or sleep, but took a casual bite of the good
things set before him and then wandered about the Palace
at untimely hours of the night, although he had a demonic
passion for the pleasures of Aphrodite?

We understand too from some of Theodora's lovers that,
while she was still on the stage, a demon of some sort swooped
on them in the night and drove them from the room where
they were spending the night with her. And there was a
dancing girl called Macedonia who belonged to the Blues
in Antioch and had acquired great influence; for by writing
letters to Justinian while Justin was still master of the Empire
she could easily destroy any she wished of prominent
citizens in eastern regions, causing their property to be confiscated for the Treasury. This woman, we are told, while
welcoming Theodora on her return from Egypt and Libya,
saw that she was very annoyed and put out by the insults
she had received at the hands of Hecebolius,[1] and by the loss
of her money during that trip. So Macedonia did her best

1. See page 85.

to console her and cheer her up, reminding her that Fortune was quite capable of playing the benefactress and showering wealth upon her. Then, we are told, Theodora declared that actually during the previous night she had had a vivid dream which told her not to worry about money any more: when she reached Byzantium she would go to bed with the King of the Demons, and would live with him as his wedded wife in every respect, and as a result would become mistress of all the money she could desire.

Such at any rate were the facts as they appeared to most people.

The character of Justinian was in the round such as I have portrayed; but he showed himself approachable and affable to those with whom he came in contact; not a single person found himself denied access to the Emperor, and even those who broke the rules by the way they stood or spoke in his presence never incurred his wrath. That, however, did not make him blush when confronting those whom he intended to destroy. In fact he never even gave a hint of anger or irritation to show how he felt towards those who had offended him; but with a friendly expression on his face and without raising an eyebrow, in a gentle voice he would order tens of thousands of quite innocent persons to be put to death, cities to be razed to the ground, and all their possessions to be confiscated for the Treasury. This characteristic would have made anybody imagine that he had the disposition of a lamb. But if anyone attempted to conciliate him and by humble supplication to beg forgiveness for those who had incurred his displeasure, then 'baring his teeth and raging like a beast'[1] he would seem to be on the

1. Quoted from Aristophanes' *Peace*.

point of bursting, so that none of his supposed intimates could nurse any further hope of persuading him to grant pardon.

He seemed to be a convinced believer in Christ, but this too meant ruin for his subjects; for he allowed the priests to use violence against their neighbours almost with impunity, and when they looted the estates next to their own he wished them joy, thinking that in doing so he was honouring the Almighty. When he tried such cases he thought that he was showing his piety if anyone for allegedly religious purposes grabbed something that did not belong to him, and after winning his case went scot-free. For in his view justice consisted in the priests' getting the better of their antagonists. And when he himself got possession by unscrupulous methods of the estates of persons living or dead, and gave these as an offering to one of the churches, he would congratulate himself on this cloak of piety – but only to make sure that ownership of these estates should not revert to those who had been robbed of them.

But he went much further, and to achieve his aim he engineered an incalculable number of murders. His ambition being to force everybody into one form of Christian belief he wantonly destroyed everyone who would not conform, and that while keeping up a pretence of piety. For he did not regard it as murder, so long as those who died did not happen to share his beliefs. Thus he had completely set his heart on the continual slaughter of his fellow-men, and together with his wife he was constantly engaged in fabricating charges in order to satisfy this ambition. The pair of them were almost indistinguishable in their aims, and where there did happen to be some real difference in their characters they were equally wicked, though they displayed exactly opposite traits in destroying their subjects. For in his judgement the Emperor was as unstable as a weathercock, at the mercy of those who at any moment wished to swing him in whatever direction they thought fit – so long as their plans did not point in the direction of generosity or unselfishness – and perpetually exposed himself to gusts of flattery. His fawning courtiers could with the utmost ease convince him that he was soaring aloft and 'walking the air'.[1]

One day as he sat beside him on the Bench, Tribonian said he was quite terrified that sooner or later as a reward for his piety the Emperor would be carried up to heaven and vanish from men's sight. Such laudations (or were they gibes?) he interpreted according to his own preconceived notions. Yet if ever by any chance he complimented some person on his virtues, a moment later he would be denouncing him as a scoundrel. On the other hand, when he had poured abuse on one of his subjects he would veer round and shower compliments on him – or so it appeared – changing about without the slightest provocation. For his thoughts ran counter to his own words and the impression he wished to give.

What his temperament was in regard to friendship and enmity I have indicated already, evidencing for the most part the man's own actions. As an enemy he was determined and undeviating, to his friends most inconstant; so that he actually brought ruin on numbers of people who had been high in his favour, but never showed friendship to any man he had once hated. Those whom he seemed to know best

1. An allusion to Socrates in Aristophanes' *Clouds*.

and to esteem most he soon betrayed, graciously presenting them to his spouse or whoever it might be, to be put to death, though he knew quite well that it was because of their devotion to himself and of that alone that they would die. For he could not be trusted in anything except inhumanity and avarice, as all the world could see: to wean him from the latter was beyond the power of any man. Why, in cases where he refused to listen even to his wife's persuasions, by throwing into the scales the hope of a big profit to be made from the business she could lead her husband by the nose into any scheme she fancied, however loudly he might protest. For if there were any ill-gotten gain in sight he was always ready to establish laws and to rescind them again. And his judicial decisions were made not in accordance with the laws he had himself enacted, but as he was led by the sight of a bigger and more splendid promise of monetary advantage. To commit a succession of petty thefts and so deprive his subjects of their property seemed to him to involve him in no discredit at all; that is to say, in cases where he could not grab the lot on some pretext or other, either by hurling an accusation out of the blue or by alleging a non-existent will.

While he ruled the Romans neither faith nor doctrine about God continued stable, no law had any permanence, no business dealings could be trusted, no contract meant anything. When he dispatched his close friends on some mission, if they happened to do away with a number of those they came up against and collect some booty, His Majesty promptly decided that they were men of real distinction and deserved to be recognized as such, since they had carried out all their instructions to the letter. But if they treated men with any clemency, when they reported back to the Court he was ill-disposed to them from then on, and indeed actively hostile; and writing off men of this kind as hopelessly old-fashioned, he called on them for no further service. The consequence was that many made strenuous efforts to convince him of their villainous character, although their regular behaviour was as different as could be. After promising certain people again and again and confirming the promise with an oath or in writing, he immediately contrived to forget it, supposing that such behaviour won him admiration. Justinian regularly behaved in this way, not only to his subjects but also to many of his enemies, as I stated earlier.[1]

He had little need of sleep as a rule, and his appetite for food and drink was unusually small: he did little more than sample a morsel, picked up with his fingertips, before leaving the table. Such things seemed to him irrelevant, as if Nature was trying to make him toe the line: time after time he went without food for two days and nights, especially when the days before the 'Easter Festival' called for such discipline. Then, as I have said, he often went two days without food and chose to live on a little water and a few wild plants, and after sleeping for perhaps one hour he would pass the rest of the night walking round and round the Palace. Yet had he been prepared to spend just that amount of time in good works, the nation could have enjoyed a very high degree of prosperity. Instead he employed all his natural powers for the ruin of the Romans, and succeeded in bringing the whole political edifice crashing to the ground. His prolonged vigils, privations, and painful efforts were

1. Book VIII.

undergone with this object alone – always and every day to devise for his subjects bigger calamities for him to crow over. For, as observed before, he was extraordinarily keen to invent and swift to execute unholy crimes, so that ultimately even the good qualities in his nature were instrumental in ruining his subjects.

All the nation's affairs were topsy-turvy, and of established customs nothing remained. I will mention a few instances, but all the rest must be passed over in silence, that my story may not go on for ever. In the first place, he himself neither possessed any quality likely to enhance the dignity of an emperor nor attempted to give the impression of possessing it: in speech, dress, and way of thinking he was utterly uncouth. Whenever he wished a decree to be published in his name, he did not send it in the usual way to the holder of the quaestor's office to be promulgated, but thought f. in most cases, in spite of the poorness of his speech, to read it out himself, supported by a large crowd of bystanders,[1] so that there was no one against whom those wronged by the decree could lodge a complaint.

The officials known as *a secretis*[2] were not allowed the privilege of writing the Emperor's secret dispatches – the task for which they had originally been appointed – but he wrote almost everything himself; for instance, whenever it was necessary to commission the city arbitrators, he would lay down the course they must follow in giving judgement. For he would not permit anybody in the Roman Empire to decide any dispute in accordance with his independent judgement, but obstinately going his own way

1. The Greek is apparently corrupt.
2. Confidential clerks.

with insane arrogance he himself settled what verdicts were to be given, accepting hearsay evidence from one of the litigants, and without proper investigation promptly cancelled decisions already given, not swayed by any law or principle of justice, but undisguisedly succumbing to sordid covetousness. For the Emperor accepted bribes without a blush, since his insatiate greed had robbed him of all sense of shame.

Frequently matters agreed between Senate and Emperor ended by being settled quite differently. The Senate sat merely as a picturesque survival, without any power either to register a decision or to do any good, assembling for the sake of appearance and in fulfilment of an old law, since no member of that assembly was ever permitted to utter one word. The Emperor and his consort for the most part made a show of taking sides in the questions at issue, but victory went to the side upon which they had already agreed. If a man had broken the law and felt that victory was not securely his, he had only to fling more gold to this Emperor in order to obtain the passage of a law going clean contrary to all existing statutes. Then if somebody else should call for the first law, which had now been repealed, His Majesty was perfectly prepared to re-enact it and substitute it for the new one. There was nothing that remained permanently in force, but the scales of justice wandered at random all over the place, whichever way the greater mass of gold weighing them down succeeded in pulling them. The home of justice was the market-hall, though it had once been the Palace, and there sale-rooms flaunted themselves in which not only the administration of justice but the making of laws too was sold to the highest bidder.

Again, the *Referendarii*,[1] as they are called, were no longer
content to convey to the Emperor the petitions of suppliants, and merely report to the magistrates as usual what his
decision was about the petitioners. Instead they collected
from every side the 'false logic',[2] and with various impost-
ures and fallacies[3] regularly deceived Justinian, whose
temperament laid him open to such cunning arts. Then as
soon as they came out and had barred the litigants from any
contact with those with whom they themselves had con-
ferred, they proceeded to extort from these defenceless
people as much money as they needed without laying themselves open to any retaliation. The soldiers on guard at the
Palace used to place themselves alongside the arbitrators in
the Royal Portico and by brute force secure the verdicts
they wanted. At that time all with few exceptions had left
their posts and were walking just as they pleased down ways
hitherto barred to them and not to be trodden; things were
all rushing along in utter disorder and had ceased to be called
by their proper names, and the commonwealth was like
children playing 'King of the Castle'. I must leave a great
deal out, as I indicated at the beginning of this section;[4]
but I must make clear who was the first man to persuade the
Emperor to accept a bribe while sitting in the judge's seat.

There was one Leon, a native of Cilicia, madly devoted
to money-making. This Leon was the prince of flatterers
with an uncanny ability for imposing his will on the minds

1. Officials who acted as channels of communication between
emperor and client.
2. Borrowed from Aristophanes' *Clouds*.
3. Adapted from Aristophanes' *Knights*.
4. Page 110.

of the ignorant, and he possessed powers of persuasion which assisted him to turn the Emperor's crass stupidity to the destruction of his fellow-men. This man was the first to persuade Justinian to sell his judicial verdicts for money. When His Majesty once made up his mind to steal in the manner described he never looked back; this scandal went on and on and grew bigger and bigger; and anyone who had made it his aim to bring a groundless suit against some honest citizen went straight to Leon, and by agreeing that a share of the property in dispute should fall to the monarch and to Leon, he had as good as won his case, in defiance of all justice, before leaving the Palace. This business enabled Leon to pile up riches on an immense scale, and he got a great deal of land into his hands, and did more than anyone to bring the Roman State to its knees.

There was no security for those who had signed contracts, no law, no oath, no written guarantees, no legal penalty, no other safeguard whatever except to toss money into the laps of Leon and the Emperor. But not even this could ensure that Leon would continue in the same mind: he was quite prepared to sell his services to the other side as well. For since he invariably robbed both sides, it never crossed his mind that to treat with supreme indifference those who had put their trust in him and to act against their interests was in any way discreditable. In his eyes, so long as profit came his way, there was no discredit in his playing a double game.

CHAPTER 4

The Crimes of Theodora

HAVING completed our portrait of Justinian, let us turn now to Theodora. Her mind was firmly and perpetually fixed upon inhumanity. No one ever once persuaded her or forced her to do anything: she herself with stubborn self-will fulfilled her own purposes with all the powers at her disposal, and nobody dared to ask mercy for anyone who had incurred her displeasure. Neither the passage of time, nor surfeit of punishment, nor any kind of appeal, nor any threat of death,[1] though all mankind lives in expectation that it will fall from heaven, could induce her to abate her wrath in the slightest. To put it in a nutshell, Theodora was never once known to come to terms with anyone who had aroused her ire, even when he had departed this life. The dead man's heir inherited the hatred of the Empress like anything else belonging to his father, and bequeathed it to the third generation. For her animosity was ever ready to be aroused to the destruction of other people, and no power on earth could mitigate it.

To her bodily needs she devoted quite unnecessary attention, though never enough to satisfy herself. She was in a great hurry to get into her bath, and very unwilling to get out again. When she had finished her ablutions she would go down to breakfast, and after a light breakfast she would take a rest. But at lunch and supper she indulged her taste for every kind of food and drink. Again and again she would

1. Theodora suffered from cancer.

sleep for hours on end, by day till nightfall and by night till
sunrise. And though she had strayed thus into every path of
self-indulgence for so great a part of the day, she thought
fit to run the whole of the Roman Empire! If the Emperor
entrusted any business to a man without first seeking her
approval, such a change of fortune would come upon that
man's affairs that very soon after he would be removed from
his position with the utmost ignominy, and die a most
shameful death.

Justinian found it easy to cope with everything, not only
because of his tranquil temperament, but because, as remarked before, he had little need of sleep as a rule, and was
approachable in the extreme. For there was almost complete
freedom for people, even if they were obscure or completely unknown, not only to come into the presence of this
autocratic monarch, but to converse with him quite freely
and be closeted with him in private. But to the Empress's
presence even for one of the magistrates there was no admission except at the cost of much time and effort; on every
occasion they all had to await her pleasure, waiting like
slaves in a small, stuffy anteroom all the time. For it was
impossibly risky for any of the magistrates to be missing.
Hour after hour they stood on tiptoes, each straining to hold
his head higher than those near him in order to catch the
eye of any eunuchs emerging from within. At long last and
after days of waiting a few of them were called for: they went
into her presence trembling with fear and hurried out again
as quickly as they could, having merely prostrated themselves and touched the instep of each imperial foot with the
edge of their lips. To make any comment or request un-
bidden by her was completely ruled out. The nation had

become a community of slaves with Theodora as slave-driver. To such an extent was the Roman State being brought to nothing, what with the monarch's temperament, which seemed too easy-going, and Theodora's, which was harsh and implacable. For an easy-going temperament meant instability, an implacable one made action impossible.

If in their attitude of mind and in their way of life they clearly had nothing in common, they were as one in their rapacity, their lust for blood, and their utter contempt for the truth. Both of them were most practised liars, and if anyone who had aroused Theodora's ire was alleged to be committing any offence however trivial and insignificant, she promptly fabricated charges which had nothing to do with the accused, and blew the matter up to criminal proportions. Endless indictments received a hearing, and a special court was established to dispose of them.[1] The juries impannelled were of Theodora's choosing, and the members were expected to contend with each other to see which of them by the inhumanity of his verdict could succeed better than the others in satisfying the Empress's desire. Thus she saw to it that the property of anyone who had offended her should be immediately pocketed by the Treasury, and after having him most cruelly flogged, though he might perhaps be descended from a long line of noble ancestors, she did not hesitate to punish him with either banishment or death. But if by any chance one of her favourites was known to have committed homicide or any other capital offence, she mocked and ridiculed the efforts of the accusers, and forced them much against their will to keep silence about what had occurred.

1. The Greek is unintelligible, and no emendation is convincing.

Again, when the fancy took her, she amused herself by turning the most serious matters into a subject for laughter, as if she were watching a comedy on the stage. For instance there was one of the patricians, an old man who had long held public office. I am well aware of his name, but I shall on no account mention it for fear of keeping alive indefinitely the ridicule that befell him. He was unable to collect a large sum owed to him by one of the Empress's servants; so he went to Her Majesty in order to accuse the other party to the transaction and to petition her for help in securing his due. But Theodora had advance information, and gave instructions to her eunuchs that when the patrician appeared before her they were to form a circle round him and listen carefully to what she said, indicating what they must say in response. When the patrician was admitted to the women's quarters, he prostrated himself in the way she always insisted on, and as if on the point of weeping spoke thus:

'Mistress, it is painful for a patrician to be short of money. For what in other men brings sympathy and compassion is regarded as ridiculous in one of my rank. Anybody else in extreme financial difficulties can inform his creditors of his position and escape immediately from his predicament; but if a patrician should find himself unable to meet his obligations, he would be terribly ashamed to disclose his situation, and if he did disclose it he would never convince his creditors, who would think it incredible that poverty could be known in such a class of society. If he does convince them, he will inevitably suffer the most shameful and agonizing misery. Well, Mistress, I have both creditors who have lent their money to me and debtors who have borrowed mine. Those who have lent to me are perpetually pressing for payment,

and respect for my position in society makes it impossible
for me to bilk them; while those who are in my debt, not
happening to be patricians, resort to inhuman excuses. I
appeal to you therefore, I beg you and implore you to help
me secure my due and escape from my present unhappy
situation.'

Such was his statement. The lady replied by intoning,
'Patrician So-and-So'; and the chorus of eunuchs chanted
their response, 'You have a great big rupture.' When the
suppliant renewed his appeal and spoke in very much the
same terms as before, the lady repeated her former reply
and the chorus their former response, until the wretched
man gave up in despair, prostrated himself in the regulation
way, left the Palace, and returned home.

Most of the year the Empress spent her time in the suburbs
overlooking the sea, chiefly in the place called Herion.[1]
This meant a great deal of discomfort for her huge retinue
of attendants; for provisions were in short supply, and they
were exposed to dangers from the sea, especially if a storm
happened to break, or the whale[2] made a sudden attack
somewhere in the area. But their master and mistress were
indifferent to the sufferings of all men alive, so long as they
themselves could live in luxurious comfort.

Theodora's method of dealing with those who had
offended her shall be my next subject. Of course I shall
mention only a few cases, that I may not seem to be toiling
at an interminable task.

1. On the opposite side of the Bosporus.
2. Nicknamed Porphyrion, this huge creature was a danger to
shipping for half a century.

When Amalasuntha[1], in her anxiety to part company with
the Goths, made up her mind to change her whole way of
life and was thinking of migrating to Byzantium, as related
in an earlier volume,[2] Theodora reflected that the woman
was an aristocrat and a queen, besides being extremely attractive in appearance and swift as lightning to find means
to her ends, and became suspicious of her splendid and
extraordinarily masculine bearing, the fickle spirit of her
own husband giving her further cause for alarm. It was not
in trifles that she made her jealousy evident: nothing less
than to ensnare the woman and bring her to her death would
satisfy the Empress. So she forthwith induced her husband
to send Peter to Italy by himself to act as ambassador. At his
departure the Emperor gave him the instructions detailed
in the relevant chapter of my record,[3] where through fear
of the Empress it was quite impossible for me to tell the true
story of what happened. She herself gave him this single
command – to remove the woman from this world at the
earliest possible moment; and she saw to it that the man was
swept off his feet by the hope of ample rewards if he carried
out her commands. When he arrived in Italy – for man is
incapable by nature of proceeding with hesitation to a
brutal murder when he has hopes of some office, perhaps,
or of a big monetary reward – he approached Theudatus
with an offer of some sort and persuaded him to make
away with Amalasuntha.[4] As recompense he was promoted

1. Daughter of Theudoric and wife of Theudatus. Her father,
the greatest of the Gothic kings, had ruled Italy from A.D. 493 till
he died in 526, leaving her to act as regent for her son.
2. Book V.   3. Book V, iv.
4. She was strangled in her bath.

to the rank of *Magister*,[1] and became immensely powerful and hated more than any man alive. So ended the story of Amalasuntha.

In Justinian's employment was a letter-writer named Priscus, utterly villainous and as blustering as any Paphlagonian,[2] just the man to fit in with the character of his master, and only too anxious to please him in the expectation of receiving similar treatment in return. Consequently he very soon accumulated a vast fortune by very shady means. However, on the ground that he treated her with scorn and put obstacles in her way, Theodora denounced him to her husband. Her first attempts produced no result, but it was not long before she put her enemy on board a ship and dispatched him in mid-winter to a destination of her own choosing. There she had his head shaved, and though he was most unwilling compelled him to become a priest! The Emperor himself behaved as if he knew nothing at all of what was going on: he made no attempt to discover the whereabouts of Priscus, nor did he ever give him another thought, but sat in silence as if steeped in oblivion. But finding that Priscus had left a little money behind he pocketed the lot.

Suspicion fell upon Theodora of a love affair[3] with one of her servants called Areobindus, of foreign extraction but handsome and quite young, whom she had chosen to be her steward. Wishing to refute the charge (though, if report was true, madly in love with the man) for the moment she

1. Commander of the Palace Guard.
2. An allusion to a punning gibe often applied by Aristophanes to Cleon.
3. The probable meaning of a corrupt passage.

made up her mind to have him cruelly flogged for no reason at all. What happened to him after that we have no idea, nor has anybody seen him to this day. For if she chose to conceal anything that was going on, that thing remained unspoken and no reference was ever made to it; the man who knew the facts was no longer allowed to report them to any of his closest friends, nor might the man who wished to learn them ask any questions, however curious he might be. Since man's first appearance on the earth no despot has ever been regarded with such fear. No one who had given offence stood any chance of escaping detection: an army of spies kept her informed of all that was said or done in the forum and in private houses. In cases where she did not wish the punishment of the offender to be generally known, this is what she used to do. She first sent for the man; then if he happened to be a person of position, she would with the strictest secrecy hand him over to one of her attendants, with instructions to convey him to the farthest limits of the Roman Empire. At dead of night the attendant would put the offender on board ship shrouded and fettered, and go on board with him. Then at the place which the Empress had appointed he would furtively hand him over to someone well qualified for this task, impressing on him that he must keep the prisoner absolutely safe, and forbidding him to say a word to anyone until the Empress felt sorry for the unfortunate creature, or after dying by inches and wasting away for many years as a result of the hardships which he suffered there he reached the end of his days. Then the attendant would set off for home.

Vasianus again, one of the Greens, a young man of some distinction, made such uncomplimentary remarks about her that she was furious with him. News of her displeasure soon came to his ears, so he took refuge in the Church of the Archangel.[1] She at once detailed the officer in charge of the people to deal with him, not giving him any instructions to charge Vasianus with his uncomplimentary remarks, but accusing him of offences against boys. The officer soon had the man out of the church and tortured him with an un-endurable form of punishment. When the people saw a member of the upper classes who had been surrounded with luxury all his life overwhelmed with such agonies, they were immediately cut to the heart, and their groans and shrieks rose to high heaven as they pleaded for the young man. But Theodora made his punishment even worse: she had his privy member cut off and destroyed him, though he had never been brought to trial, and finished by confiscating his estate for the Treasury. Thus whenever this harpy worked herself up no sanctuary was inviolate, no law offered any protection, nor was the intercession of a city's entire population sufficient to save the offender from his doom, nor could anything else on earth overcome her determination.

In the same way Diogenes, because he was a Green, roused Theodora's fury. He was a charming fellow, very popular with everyone, including the Emperor himself, but that fact did not weaken her determination to charge him slanderously with offences against male persons. She suborned two of his household slaves, and produced them in court to serve both as prosecutors and as witnesses against their owner. He was not examined secretly and behind locked doors, as was usual with her, but in open court, a large jury being chosen from men with excellent qualifications, in

1. St Michael.

deference to the high standing of Diogenes. The jury, after investigating the case with great thoroughness, came to the conclusion that the evidence of the slaves was not weighty enough to enable them to reach a verdict, especially as the witnesses were mere boys. So the Empress locked up Theodore, one of Diogenes's closest friends, in her favourite cells. There she set about her victim with many flattering enticements, and finally with prolonged physical torture. Since this treatment produced no result, she ordered a strip of leather to be wound round the prisoner's head about his ears and then twisted and tightened. Theodore imagined that his eyes had left their sockets and jumped out of his head; but he resolutely declined to confess anything that he had not done. Accordingly the jury ruled that the evidence had failed to substantiate the charge and found the accused Not Guilty, and the city with one accord kept holiday in honour of the event.

That was the end of this story. At the beginning of the present volume I described what Belisarius and Photius and Buzes suffered at her hands.

Two Blue partisans of Cilician origin, at the head of a riotous crowd, set upon Callinicus, the Governor of the Second Cilicia, and subjected him to physical assault. His groom, who was standing by his side and tried to shield his master, was murdered before the eyes of the Governor and the whole populace. The partisans were convicted of a series of murders culminating in this one, and in accordance with the law the governor sentenced them to death; but when Theodora heard of it she flaunted her support of the Blues by seizing Callinicus while still in office, and without the slightest pretext impaling him over the murderers' grave. The Emperor shed crocodile tears over the dead governor and sat there grunting like a pig,[1] and though he uttered dire threats against those who had executed the outrage he did nothing at all. But the property of the dead man he plundered without the slightest hesitation.

Theodora made it her business also to devise punishments for the sins of the flesh. Prostitutes – more than five hundred in all – were rounded up; women who in the middle of the forum sold their services for a shilling a time, just enough to keep body and soul together. They were then dispatched to the mainland opposite and confined in the Convent known as Repentance in an attempt to force them into a better way of life. However, some of them from time to time threw themselves down from the parapet during the night, and so escaped being transmogrified against their will.

In Byzantium, there were two young sisters. Not only had their father – and his father and grandfather before him – attained the consulship, but their remote ancestors had been some of the most distinguished members of the Senate. These girls had already been married, but the unfortunate deaths of their husbands had left them widowed. Thereupon Theodora picked out two vulgar, revolting creatures with the firm intention of marrying them to the girls, whom she accused of improper living. Terrified by this prospect they took refuge in the Church of Sophia, and making for the holy baptistery held on to the font with their hands. But such privations and sufferings did the Empress inflict upon them that in their anxiety to escape from the miseries of their confinement they became reconciled to the lesser evil of

1. Borrowed from Aristophanes' *Acharnians*.

the proposed marriage. So true it was that for Theodora no place remained unsullied or inviolate. Thus these girls were coerced into matrimony with a pair of beggarly louts far beneath them in station, though there were young aristocrats who would have been delighted to marry them. Their mother, a widow herself, dared not voice her grief or shed a tear over their calamity, but steeled herself to attend the betrothal. Later Theodora, anxious to shake off the guilt of her loathsome conduct, resolved to make amends to the young wives at the cost of injury to the community. She bestowed an office of authority on each of the husbands. But the girls found no consolation even in this, and incurable, intolerable distresses were brought by these men on almost all their subordinates, as I shall show in a later volume.[1] For Theodora had no respect either for office or for the common weal, nor did anything else matter to her so long as she accomplished her purpose.

Now it happened that while she was still on the stage Theodora had become pregnant by one of her lovers, and being unusually slow to recognize her unfortunate condition she tried by all her usual means to procure an abortion; but try as she might she could not get rid of the untimely infant, since by now it was not far from acquiring perfect human shape. So as she was achieving nothing, she was compelled to abandon her efforts and give birth to the child. When the baby's father saw that she was upset and annoyed because now that she was a mother she would no longer be able to employ her body as before, he rightly suspected that she would resort to infanticide; so he took up the child in acknowledgement that it was his and named it John, since

1. See footnote on page 41.

it was a boy. Then he went off to Arabia for which he was bound. When he himself was on the point of death and John was now in his early teens, the boy learnt from his father's lips the whole story about his mother; and when his father departed this life, performed all the customary rites over him. A little while later he came to Byzantium, and made his arrival known to those who at all times had access to his mother. They, never imagining that she would feel any differently from the generality of mankind, reported to the mother that her son John had arrived. Fearing that the story would come to the ears of her husband, Theodora gave instructions that the boy was to come into her presence. When he appeared, she took one look at him and put him in the hands of one of her personal attendants whom she regularly entrusted with such commissions. By what means the poor lad was removed from the world of the living I am unable to say, but no one to this day has ever set eyes on him, even since the decease of the Empress.

At that period almost all women had become morally depraved. For they could play false to their husbands with complete impunity, since such behaviour involved them in no danger or harm. Wives proved guilty of adultery were exempt from penalty, as they had only to go straight to the Empress and turn the tables by bringing a countersuit against their husbands, who had not been charged with any offence, and dragging them into court. All that was left to the husbands, against whom nothing had been proved, was to pay twice the amount of the dowry they had received, and as a rule to be scourged and led away to prison – and then once more to watch their faithless partners showing off and inviting the attentions of their paramours more brazenly than before. Many of the paramours actually gained promotion by rendering this service. Small wonder that from then on most husbands, however shocking their wives' behaviour might be, were only too glad to keep their mouths shut and avoid being scourged, conceding every licence to their wives by letting them believe that they had not been found out.

The Empress felt herself entitled to assume control of every branch of public affairs according to her own personal ideas. It was she who filled the offices of Church and State, investigating one point alone and invariably insisting that no honourable or good man should be a candidate for high office; no one in fact who would be incapable of giving effect to her instructions. Again, she arranged all marriages as if by divine right. In her time no contracts of marriage were voluntarily entered into: a man would suddenly discover that he had a wife, not because he had any desire for one, which is the one thing that matters even in backward countries. but because Theodora willed it. The women thus pushed into marriage found themselves in the same disagreeable situation: they were forced to live with men when they had not the slightest inclination that way. Often the Empress would even fetch the bride out of the bridal chamber at a mere whim, leaving the bridegroom still unmarried, and merely declaring in a fit of anger that she disapproved of the match. Among the large number of men whom she treated in this way were Leontius, who occupied the position of *Referendarius*, and Saturninus, son of Hermogenes the *Magister*, both of them just married.

This Saturninus had married a second cousin, a maiden of good birth and excellent character, whose father Cyril had

approved the match, Hermogenes having died earlier. No
sooner had they shut themselves into the bridal chamber
than Theodora seized the groom and carried him off to
another chamber, where in spite of his heartbroken protesta-
tions he was married to Chrysomallo's daughter. This
Chrysomallo had once been a dancer and later a courtesan,
but at the time of this incident she was living in the Palace
with another Chrysomallo and Indaro. For there it was that
after abandoning woman's oldest profession and the life of
the theatre they had established their headquarters. When
Saturninus had slept with his new bride and found that she
had been deflowered, he informed one of his intimate
friends that the girl he had married was nothing but damaged
goods. When this comment came to Theodora's ears, she
said that he was showing off and had no right to be so puffed
up, and ordered her servants to bend him over like any
schoolboy. Then she gave his behind a fearsome beating
and told him not to talk such nonsense in future.

What she did to John the Cappadocian has been related in
an earlier volume.[1] Her actions sprang from her anger
against him, which was not due to his offences against the
State – she proved this later, when men who treated those
under them more outrageously still in no case received such
punishment at her hands – but to the boldness he showed in
standing up to her in one matter after another, and above all
to the damaging accusation which he brought against her
to the Emperor, with the result that she and her husband
were almost in a state of open war. As I said at the start, in
this book I must at all costs make clear the true reasons for
what happened.

1. Book I.

When she had locked him up in Egypt after he had undergone all the miseries already described in my pages, even then she was not satisfied with the punishments she had inflicted on him, but kept up a relentless search for false witnesses to bring against him. Four years later she managed to find two Greens belonging to the party in Cyzicus: they were believed to have taken part in the revolt against the bishop.[1] By means of flattery, arguments, and threats she got these two so firmly in her power that one of them, terrified and at the same time elated with expectations of profit, laid the horrible responsibility for the bishop's murder on the shoulders of John. The other man flatly refused to speak anything but the truth, even though he was stretched on the rack till he seemed certain to die at any moment. And so she was completely baffled in her efforts to get rid of John on this pretext; yet she cut off the right hands of these two young men – of one because he could not be coerced into giving false evidence; of the other for fear her scheming might become clear as daylight. And although all this was going on in the forum with no attempt at concealment, her husband pretended that he knew nothing whatever about it.

1. Eusebius, Bishop of Cyzicus.

CHAPTER 5

The Destruction Wrought by a Demon-Emperor

THAT the emperor was not a man but, as I have already pointed out, a demon in human shape, could be demonstrated by considering the magnitude of the calamities which he brought on the human race. For it is by the immensity of what he accomplishes that the power of the doer is manifested. To make any accurate estimate of the number of lives destroyed by this man would never, it seems to me, be within the power of any living being other than God. For sooner could one number all the sands than the hosts of men destroyed by this potentate. But making a rough estimate of the area which has been denuded of its inhabitants I suggest that a million million lost their lives. Libya, for instance, in spite of its enormous size, has been laid so utterly waste that however far one went it would be a difficult and remarkable achievement to find a single person there. Yet the Vandals who took part in the recent armed revolt in that country were eighty thousand strong, and the number of their women and children and slaves can hardly be guessed. As for the Libyans who had once lived in the cities and farmed the land or toiled on the sea – as I know only too well since I saw it with my own eyes – how could any man on earth begin to estimate their vast numbers? And even they were few in comparison with the Moorish inhabitants, who perished to a man along with their wives and little ones. Furthermore, many of the Roman soldiers and many of those who had accompanied them from Byzantium lie under the earth. Thus if one insisted that in Libya alone five million people lost their lives, he would, I suspect, be understating the facts. The reason was that as soon as the Vandals had been crushed Justinian took no steps to tighten his hold over the country, and made no plans to ensure that its resources should be secured for him by winning the firm loyalty of the inhabitants. Instead he immediately instructed Belisarius to return home without loss of time, accusing him of political ambitions of which he was entirely innocent, so that from then on he could order things at his own sweet will and swallow up all the plunder of Libya.

He immediately sent out assessors, if you please, to value the land, and imposed crushing taxation unknown before, and assumed the ownership of all the most valuable estates. Then he turned his attention to the Arians, whom he debarred from celebrating their customary sacraments. Finally he kept his armed forces waiting for their pay, and in other ways made life a burden for his soldiers. The result of all this was an outbreak of revolts that led to widespread destruction. For he could never bring himself to let well alone: he had an innate passion for throwing everything into confusion and chaos.

Italy, which is at least three times as large as Libya, has been far more completely depopulated than the latter; so proof of the scale of destruction there too will not be far to seek. The responsibility for what happened in Italy has already been made clear in an earlier chapter.[1] All the blunders that he made in Libya had their counterparts here. And by sending his audit-officers, as they are called, to swell

1. Book VII, xxiii.

the staff on the spot, he instantly overturned and ruined everything.

Before this war began, the Gothic Empire stretched from Gaul to the boundaries of Dacia, where stands the city of Sirmium. Gaul and Venetia were for the most part in German occupation at the time when the Roman army arrived in Italy. Sirmium and its neighbourhood are in the hands of the Gepaides; but all this region, roughly speaking, is completely depopulated. For some died in the war, others succumbed to disease and starvation, which war inevitably brings in its train. Illyricum and the whole of Thrace – that is to say, from the Ionian Gulf to the suburbs of Byzantium, an area which includes Greece and the Chersonnese – were overrun almost every year by Huns, Slavs, and Antae, from the day that Justinian took charge of the Roman Empire. In these raids the local inhabitants suffered untold miseries. I believe that in every incursion more than two hundred thousand of the Romans residing there were killed or enslaved, so that the whole region was turned into a second Scythian desert.[1]

Such were the consequences of the wars in Libya and in Europe. All this time the Saracens were continuously overrunning Roman territory in the East from Egypt to the frontiers of Persia, doing their deadly work so thoroughly that the whole of that region was left almost uninhabited: I do not think it possible that any human being, however careful his investigations, will ever find out the numbers of those who perished in these raids. Again, the Persians under Chosroes thrice invaded the rest of the Roman territory and razed the cities to the ground. Of the men and women they

1. An allusion to Aristophanes' *Acharnians*.

captured in the cities that they stormed and in the various country districts, some they butchered, others they carried away with them, leaving the land completely uninhabited wherever they happened to swoop. And from the time when they first invaded Colchis the destruction of the Colchians, the Lazi, and the Romans has continued to this day.

However, neither Persians nor Saracens nor Huns, nor the Slav peoples nor any other foreign invaders, were lucky enough to withdraw from Roman soil unscathed. During their incursions, and still more during sieges and battles, they came up against many obstacles and their casualties were as heavy as their enemies'. For not only Romans but nearly all the nations outside their borders had the benefit of Justinian's bloodthirstiness. As if Chosroes was not a bad enough character himself, Justinian, as I made clear in the appropriate part of my book,[1] provided him with every inducement to go to war. For he took no pains to fit his actions to the circumstance of the moment, but did everything at the wrong time. In time of peace or truce he was always treacherously contriving pretexts for aggression against his neighbours; in time of war he slackened off in the most foolish way, showing a woeful lack of energy in preparing for the projected operations, simply because he hated to part with his money. Instead of giving his mind to the task in hand he went in for stargazing and for foolish attempts to determine the nature of God: he would not abandon the war because he was bloodthirsty and murderous by nature, nor could he overcome his enemies because sheer meanness prevented him from tackling the essential problems. Is it surprising that while he was on the throne

1. Book I, xxiii.

the whole earth reeked of human blood, shed in an unending stream both by the Romans and by nearly all the peoples outside their borders?

Such, in fine, was the toll of the wars that took place at this time in all parts of the Empire. And when I reckon up the toll of the civil strife that took place in Byzantium and every city besides, my conclusion is that as many lives were lost in this way as in the wars. Justice and impartial punishment for crimes committed were hardly ever seen, and the Emperor gave enthusiastic support to one of the two parties; so naturally their rivals did not lie down either. They all took to desperate courses, utterly heedless of the consequences, the one side because they were the underdogs, the other side because they were on top. Sometimes they went for each other *en masse*, sometimes they fought in small groups, or again, from time to time they laid traps for individual opponents; and for thirty-two years they never missed one opportunity of practising frightful brutalities against each other, while at the same time they were constantly being sentenced to death by the magistrate responsible for public order. But even so, punishment for the crimes committed fell almost entirely on the Greens. We may add that punitive action against Samaritans and so-called heretics filled the Roman Empire with blood. This brief sketch is all that I propose to offer now: I gave a sufficiently detailed account two chapters back.[1]

1. It is impossible to say how many lives were lost during Justinian's reign. Gibbon thought that the number might have approached a hundred million. Procopius's *million million* (literally *ten thousand times ten thousand times ten thousand*) is no more intended to be taken literally than is St John's *ten thousand times ten thousand, and thousands of thousands*, or the *thousands of ten thousands* of Rebekah's progeny.

Such were the disasters which in the time of this demon in human form befell the entire human race, disasters for which Justinian as the reigning emperor must bear the responsibility. The immeasurable distress which some hidden power and demonic nature enabled him to bring upon his fellow-men will be the next subject of my story. For while this man was at the head of affairs there was a continuous series of catastrophes, which as some maintained were due to the presence here of this wicked demon and to his machinations, though others argued that the Deity, hating all that Justinian did and turning His back on the Roman Empire, had given the avenging demons licence to work all the mischief that I am about to describe.

To begin with, the River Scirtus inundated Edessa, bringing on the inhabitants calamities without number, which I shall recount in a later volume.[1] Next, the Nile rose in the usual way but failed to sink again at the proper time, bringing upon some of the inhabitants sufferings which I described earlier.[2] Thirdly, the Cydnus poured almost all round Tarsus, inundated the city for days on end, and did not subside until it had done incalculable damage there. Again, earthquakes destroyed Antioch, the first city of the East, Seleucia, which is its nearest neighbour, and Anazarbus, the most famous city in Cilicia. The number of lives lost in these three cities it is impossible to estimate; and we must not forget Ibora and Amasia, the first city in Pontus, or Polybotus in Phrygia, and the town which the Pisidians call Philomede, or Lychnidus in Epirus, and Corinth, all of which had had huge populations for centuries past. Every

1. *Buildings*, Book II.
2. Book VII.

one of these cities has been overthrown by an earthquake during this short period, and the inhabitants almost without exception have perished with them. On top of the earthquakes came the epidemic which I mentioned before;[1] this carried off about half the survivors. On such a vast scale was the loss of life, first while this man was acting as Head of the State, and later when he reigned as monarch.

I shall now go on to relate how he appropriated all the money he could lay his hands on, first mentioning a dream-vision which at the beginning of Justin's reign appeared to a citizen of high rank. He told how in his dream he had fancied that he was standing somewhere in Byzantium on the sea shore exactly opposite Chalcedon, and that he saw Justinian standing in front of him right in the middle of the channel. First Justinian drank up all the water of the sea, so that from then on he seemed to the dreamer to be standing on dry land, as the waves did not break on the shore at this point; then other water appeared there, choked with masses of filth and rubbish and pouring out of sewers on both sides. This Justinian drank up as well, laying bare once more the bed of the channel. This was what the man saw in his dream-vision.

When Justin ascended the throne, his nephew Justinian found the government's coffers full of public money. For Anastasius had shown himself the most provident and economical of all the emperors, and fearing – with good cause – that his successor might find himself short of money and be tempted to plunder his subjects, he had filled all the

1. Book II.

treasuries to the doors with gold before he reached the end of his days. All this Justinian dissipated in next to no time, partly on constructions on the shore which served no useful purpose, partly on largesse to tribes outside the Empire. Yet one would have expected it to keep the most extravagant of emperors amply provided for a hundred years. For it was emphatically stated by the officials in charge of the funds and treasuries and all other forms of imperial wealth that Anastasius, after reigning over the Romans for more than twenty-seven years, had left gold to the value of £48,000,000 in the state coffers. But in the nine short years of Justin's reign this man Justinian created such confusion and disorder in the body politic that no less than £60,000,000 was brought into the Imperial Treasury by improper means; yet nothing whatever was left of all that accumulated wealth: while Justin was still alive this spendthrift squandered the lot in the manner already described.[1] As to the sums which in his lifetime he managed to appropriate to himself illegally and then expend, there is no possible way of accounting for them or estimating their magnitude. Like an overflowing river he daily ravaged and despoiled his subjects; but the whole flood swept straight on to enrich the natural enemies of his country.

As soon as he had denuded the country of all its public wealth, he turned his eyes towards his individual subjects, and lost no time in stripping most of them of their estates, which he seized by main force with no attempt at justification. Though no charges had been brought, he hauled up those who were thought to be well off in Byzantium and in every city besides. Some he accused of polytheism, some

1. See page 77.

of professing unorthodox beliefs about Christ, some of offences against boys, others of love-affairs with nuns or other improper forms of intercourse, others of provoking faction-fights, or of attachment to the Green party, or of disloyalty to himself, or of anything else in the catalogue of crimes. Another trick was by a stroke of the pen to make himself heir of deceased persons, or even of the living if he saw a chance, on the ground that they had adopted him. These were his most distinguished efforts. The way in which he turned to his own advantage the insurrection against him known as 'Nika', and immediately became heir of every senator, I explained a little way back;[1] also the way in which before the insurrection he had appropriated to himself, one at a time, the estates of a considerable number of them.

On all his country's potential enemies he lost no opportunity of lavishing vast sums of money – on those to East, West, North, and South, as far as the inhabitants of Britain and the nations in every part of the known world, nations of which not even a rumour had ever before reached our ears, and whose names we learnt only when we at last saw them with our eyes. For when they heard what sort of man Justinian was they did not wait for an invitation: from every direction they poured into Byzantium to get in touch with him. The Emperor was not in the least dismayed, but delighted at the whole business, deeming it an unexpected piece of luck to be able to ladle out Roman wealth and toss it to members of inferior races or pour it on to the waves of the sea; and day after day he continued to send them home, every one of them with masses of money. Thus it is that foreign nations on every side have come to be possessed of

1. See page 101.

all the wealth of the Romans, either by receiving the money
from the Emperor's hand, or by plundering the Roman
Empire, or by selling back their prisoners of war, or by
demanding money in return for a cease-fire. In this way the
dream-vision which I related a little way back was fulfilled
for the man who saw it.

There were yet other methods which Justinian managed
to devise for despoiling his subjects, and which without
more ado I shall describe to the best of my ability – methods
which made it perfectly simple for him to plunder the
estates of all his subjects, not all at once, but bit by bit.

First, he made it his practice to give authority over the
people in Byzantium to a prefect who was to take a half share
of the annual profits of the shopkeepers in return for giving
them permission to sell their wares at whatever price they
liked. Consequently the customers who did their household
shopping there had to pay three times the proper price, and
there was no one to whom they could complain about it.
This scandal was productive of a great deal of harm. For as
the Treasury collected a share of these profits, the official
responsible for these matters was only too pleased to enrich
himself from this source. In the next place the subordinates
to whom the official had delegated these unsavoury duties,
joining forces with the shopkeepers, grasped with both
hands this freedom to break the law, and treated abominably
those who had to do their shopping then or not at all, not
only collecting, as has been said, monstrously inflated prices,
but practising unspeakable frauds in the quality of the
commodities sold.

His second step was to establish a number of monopolies,
as they are called, selling the welfare of his subjects to those

who were prepared to operate this monstrous system. He himself went off with the payment which he had exacted as his share of the bargain, while those who had come to this arrangement with him were allowed to run their business just as they pleased. He behaved in the same unscrupulous way without any attempt at concealment in dealing with all the other magistracies. The Emperor always pocketed his own little share of their ill-gotten gains; so the magistrates and those immediately responsible for each piece of jobbery plunged all the more recklessly into the plundering of all who came into their power.

As if the historic magistracies were not adequate for this purpose of his, he invented two additional ones for the management of public business, though hitherto all indictments had been dealt with by the magistrate responsible for public order. But to ensure that the number of professional informers should be constantly increasing, and to facilitate yet further the subjection of perfectly inoffensive persons to physical ill-usage, he made up his mind to create these two new offices. The holder of one was appointed supposedly to bring thieves to justice, receiving the title of Praetor of the Plebeians; the holder of the other was charged with the correction of habitual offenders against boys and of those who had illicit intercourse with women, and of those again who did not show orthodox reverence for the Deity. This official received the title of *Quaesitor*. Now note what happened. The Praetor, if among the stolen goods he put his hand on any articles of great value, made it his business to hand these to the Emperor, explaining that it was impossible to discover their owners. In this way His Majesty always contrived to secure a share of the most valuable plunder. The one called *Quaesitor*, when he had finished with alleged offenders, would hand over as much as he thought fit, without seriously impairing his capacity to enrich himself illegally at the expense of other people. For the subordinates of these magistrates never produced any accusers, and never called anyone to give evidence of the alleged offences, but through all this time the long line of those unlucky enough to fall into their clutches, though neither accused nor proved guilty, were with the utmost secrecy murdered and stripped of their property.

Later this bloodthirsty devil instructed these officials and the magistrate responsible for public order to deal indiscriminately with all accusations, telling them to compete with each other to find out which of them could destroy the biggest number in the shortest time. It is said that one of them promptly asked him, if one day someone were to be denounced to all three of them, which one should have the handling of the case. The answer came at once – whichever of them got his nose in first.

Again, he meddled most improperly with the office of the magistrate called the Quaestor, an office which had been treated with the greatest respect by previous emperors almost without exception, who saw to it that the highest standard of general experience, and above all of skill in legal matters, should be required in holders of this office, who must in addition be manifestly incapable of accepting a bribe; for the consequences would be calamitous for the State if holders of this office were either hampered by any want of experience or given up to avarice. This emperor on the other hand began by appointing to this office Tribonian, whose activities were described in detail in an earlier

volume.[1] When Tribonian departed this life Justinian purloined a slice of his estate, although he had left a son and a
number of grandchildren when he was overtaken by his last
day on earth. Junilus, a Libyan by race, was chosen to fill
the vacancy, though he had not even a nodding acquaintance
with the law, since he was not even one of the recognized
pleaders. He had a good knowledge of Latin, but as regards
Greek he had never even been to school and could not get
his tongue round the language – why, often when he did his
best to pronounce a Greek word he moved his subordinates
to scornful laughter. He had an overwhelming passion for
making money in dirty ways: he actually put documents
signed by the Emperor up to public auction without turning
a hair; and in return for a single gold coin he unblushingly
held out his palm to all and sundry. For a period of
seven whole years these goings on made the State an
object of ridicule. When Junilus too came to the end of
his days the Emperor gave this office to Constantine, who
had had some training in the law, but was absurdly young
and had had no experience hitherto of lawyers' wrangles;
and he was the biggest thief and the biggest boaster
alive.

This man had wormed his way deep into Justinian's
affections and had become one of his dearest friends: at no
time did the Emperor hesitate to use him as a tool either in
stealing or in manipulating the law-courts. So it was not
long before Constantine made a pile of money and became
unbearably pompous, 'walking the air and contemplating

1. Book I. Tribonian was an able and learned man largely responsible for the codification of Roman law. Procopius portrays
him as extremely avaricious.

the entire human race with scorn'.[1] If people were prepared
to hand over a great deal of money to him, they had to
deposit it with some of his most trusted assistants; then they
were free to put into effect the plans they had at heart. But
to meet the quaestor himself or to have any contact with
him was impossible for anyone at all, unless he caught him
running to the Palace or returning from there – never at a
walk, but in haste and at a great speed, to make sure that
those who came near him did not waste his time without
paying for it.

Such were the methods of Justinian in this sphere of his
operations. If we turn now to the Praetorian Prefect, we
find that every year he levied more than £450,000 on top
of the regular taxes. To this impost he gave the name 'sky
tax' – to show, I suppose, that this was not a regular or
permanent tax, but that by some lucky chance it always
seemed to drop out of the sky into his lap. These practices
might better be described as an exhibition of his villainy. In
the name of this tax holders of this office grew continually
bolder in their plundering of the common people. The
proceeds were supposed to be handed over to the Emperor,
but the officers acquired a princely fortune for themselves
without the slightest trouble. Justinian, however, saw no
need to take the least notice of such things: he looked for
the day when they had made a really big pile; for then he
could at once bring against them some charge or other to
which there was no answer, and there would be nothing to
prevent him from depriving them at one stroke of everything they possessed. This was the treatment that he meted
out to John the Cappadocian.

1. A second reminiscence of the description of Socrates in the *Clouds*.

Everyone, of course, who occupied this position during the period in question suddenly found himself rich beyond his dreams. There were just two exceptions. One was Phocas, whom I described in an earlier volume[1] as a man of unshakeable integrity: he resisted all temptation to enrich himself while in office. The other was Bassus, who did not assume the office till a later date. But neither of these two retained the position for a single year: on the ground that they were useless and quite out of touch with the age they lived in they were ousted from their position within a few months. But I must not go into minute detail and drag my story out interminably: I need only say that the same things were going on in all the other ministries in Byzantium.

Everywhere in the Roman Empire Justinian followed this method. He picked out the most degraded specimens of humanity he could lay his hands on and sold them the offices they were to corrupt, charging a very high price; for no one with any decency or any vestige of good sense would ever think of pouring out his own money for the pleasure of robbing inoffensive citizens. After collecting the cash from those with whom he was negotiating he gave them permission to do anything they liked to those under them. This enabled them to ruin all the districts allotted to them, inhabitants and all, and make enough money to keep them in luxury for the rest of their lives. To find the money to pay for their cities they obtained a loan from the bank at a very high rate of interest and handed over the money to the vendor; then when they arrived in the cities, from then on they brought every variety of misery upon their subjects, having no other object in life than to make sure that they

1. Book I.

could satisfy their creditors, and themselves be included
from then on amongst the richest in the land. The business
did not lay them open to any risk or criticism; it brought
them on the contrary a good deal of admiration, which
became greater and greater as they succeeded in the senseless
killing and despoiling of more and more of their chance
victims. For to call them murderers and despoilers was to
give them credit for vigour and effectiveness. But the
moment that Justinian noticed that any office-holder had
amassed a fortune, he found some excuse for netting him
and dropping him and all he possessed into his creel.

Later he made a law that candidates for offices must swear
that they would faithfully keep their own hands clean from
all thieving, and would neither give nor receive any payment in connexion with their official duties. And he laid
all the curses that have come down from the distant past on
anyone who broke the written agreements. But the law
had been in force less than a year when he himself, scorning
agreements and oaths and the disgrace involved, began with
less hesitation than ever to bargain about the prices of the
various offices, not in some dark corner but in the open
forum. Naturally those who bought the offices, regardless
of their oath, looted right and left more recklessly than
before.

Later still he contrived yet another scheme, quite breath-
taking. Those offices which he considered the most important in Byzantium and the other cities he decided that he
would not continue to sell as before. Instead he sought out
hirelings to fill the vacancies, arranging with them that in
return for a salary of some kind they should hand over to
him all the loot. They, on receiving their salary, blithely set

to work collecting and carrying off everything from the whole countryside, and a hireling authority went out in all directions plundering the ordinary people in the name of the office. In this way the Emperor, choosing with the greatest care, all the time put in charge of affairs those who without any doubt were the biggest scoundrels in the world, and always managed to track down this loathsome quarry. In fact, when he installed the first batch of scoundrels in office and the licence which power gave them brought their evil dispositions to light, we were utterly astounded that human nature could find room for such immense wickedness. But when in the course of time their places were taken by others who were able to go far beyond them, people began to ask each other how it came about that those who a little while ago seemed the most utter scoundrels were so amazingly outdone by their successors that they now appeared to have behaved like perfect gentlemen in all their proceedings. The third batch in their turn outranged the second in every kind of iniquity, only to be followed by others who by their ingenuity in dragging people into court surrounded the memory of their predecessors with an odour of virtue. As things went from bad to worse all men came to learn by experience that man's innate wickedness knows no limit: when it feeds on the knowledge of the past, and when the licence which impunity bestows encourages it to victimize all whom it encounters, it seems to swell inevitably to such proportions that it is not even possible for the minds of the sufferers to grasp its immensity. Such were the miseries the Romans underwent at the hands of their magistrates.

Over and over again when an army of enemy Huns had plundered the Roman Empire and enslaved the inhabitants,

the Thracian and Illyrian commanders planned to attack
them as they retired; but they reversed their decision when
they were shown a letter from the Emperor Justinian forbidding them to launch their attack on the invaders, since they
were needed as allies of the Romans against the Goths, perhaps, or against some other of their enemies. The result was
that these wild tribes began to act as open enemies and to
plunder and enslave any Romans within reach; then with
their prisoners and other booty they would, in their capacity
as friends and allies of the Romans, return to their own
homes. Over and over again some of the farmers of those
parts, impelled by longing for their wives and children who
had been carried off as slaves, made a united assault on the
retreating enemy and succeeded in killing numbers of them
and capturing their horses together with all the booty – only
to find that the consequences of their action were very
painful indeed. For a body of men dispatched from Byzantium took it upon them without the slightest hesitation
to assault them and knock them about in addition to imposing fines, until they handed over all the horses which they
had taken from the raiders.

When the Emperor and Theodora had got rid of John
the Cappadocian, they wanted to appoint a successor; so
they made united and strenuous efforts to find someone
still more degraded, looking round for such an instrument
of their tyranny, and minutely investigating the temp-
eraments of the candidates, in the hope of ruining their
subjects even faster than before. For the time being they
chose Theodotus to fill John's place, not a good man by
any means, but not bad enough to fill the bill completely.

After doing so they continued their painstaking scrutiny in all directions. To their surprise they found a money-changer of Syrian origin called Peter and surnamed Barsymes. For years he had stood behind the counter changing bronze coins and making an inexcusably high profit out of the transaction, having a very clever knack of filching the halfpennies and deceiving one customer after another by the quickness of his fingers. He showed remarkable dexterity in pocketing the property of any who came his way, and if caught he instantly swore his innocence and covered up the misdemeanour of his hands with the effrontery of his tongue. He enlisted in the Imperial Guard, and charged into such horrifying courses that he delighted Theodora and helped her enthusiastically to overcome the difficulties in her own unscrupulous plans. So Theodotus, whom they had appointed to succeed the Cappadocian, was immediately relieved of his office, and replaced by Peter, who performed their wishes in every particular. He robbed the soldiers on active service of their pay and allowances without ever giving a hint of shame or fear. He even put up the local magistracies to auction more brazenly than ever before, and lowering their prestige he used to sell them to those who did not shrink from engaging in this unholy traffic, expressly authorizing purchasers of the offices to treat the lives and property of their subjects in any way they chose. For it was agreed at once between Peter and the man who had put down the price of the locality that he should have licence to plunder and pillage as he liked.

Thus from the virtual Head of the State proceeded the traffic in men's lives, and with him the bargain was struck for the destruction of the cities. Through the chief law-

courts and round the open forum strode a licensed bandit,
who defined his duties as the collection of the sums handed
over in payment for public office. There was of course no
hope that notice would be taken of his misdemeanours.
Then again, of all persons in State employment – they were
both numerous and distinguished – he invariably attracted
to himself the very worst. Such misconduct, alas, was not
practised by him alone, but by all the earlier and later
occupants of this office. The same sort of thing went on in
the department of the *Magister*, as he is called, and among
the Officers of the Household, whose duties are to attend
to all business in connexion with State finances, with the
privata,[1] as they are called, and the *patrimonium*[2] – in fact,
in all the departments centred in Byzantium and the other
cities. For from the time that this autocrat took charge of
affairs, in every department the monies earmarked for the
junior officials were commandeered without any justification, sometimes by Justinian himself, sometimes by the head
of the department. Meanwhile the men who took their
orders from them were reduced to extreme penury, and
had to work all the time as if they were the lowest of slaves.

A very large quantity of grain had been stored in Byzantium, but most of it was rotten already; so without
consulting anyone the Emperor foisted it on all the eastern
cities in proportion to their population, though it was unfit
for human consumption; and foisted it on them, not at the
normal rate for top quality grain, but at a much higher price.
After pouring out vast sums to meet these inflated charges
there was nothing that the purchasers could do except to

1. The contents of the Emperor's Privy Purse.
2. Money which the Emperor had inherited from his predecessor.

dump the grain in the sea or in a sewer. There was still a large store of sound grain that had not yet gone rotten; this too he decided to sell at top price to those cities that were at all short of grain. By this means he made a hundred per cent profit on the money which the Treasury had originally paid to the tributary states for this grain.

The next year, however, the harvest of the fields was not nearly so abundant, and the grain fleet arrived at Byzantium with quite inadequate supplies. So Peter, not knowing how to deal with the situation, thought it best to buy a great quantity of grain from places in Bithynia, Phrygia, and Thrace. The inhabitants of these regions had no option but to undertake the heavy task of carrying the cargoes down to the coast and to face the dangers involved in transportng them to Byzantium, where they received from him a derisory sum in so-called settlement. Their loss amounted to such a huge total that they would have been glad if they had been allowed to deposit the grain in a government warehouse gratis, and to pay an additional sum for the privilege. This is the burden commonly referred to as 'requisition'. But even so there was still insufficient grain in Byzantium to meet the demand, and many people protested vigorously to the Emperor about the business. At the same time almost all the men in the armed forces, as they had not received the pay to which they were entitled, gave themselves up to disorder and constant rioting all over the city.

The Emperor now made it clear that he was dissatisfied with Peter: he wished to remove him from office, both for the reasons mentioned and because he had been informed that Peter had salted away a fantastic amount of public money which he had managed to embezzle. The information was true enough. But Theodora refused to let her husband do this; for she was extraordinarily attached to Barsymes, apparently because of his sheer badness and his more than brutal treatment of those under him. She herself, of course, was utterly ruthless and full to bursting with inhumanity, and she expected her subordinates to be as like herself as possible in character. They say that she was bewitched by Peter and compelled against her will to show him favour; for sorcerers and demons were an obsession with this man Barsymes, and he was lost in admiration of the Manichees,[1] as they are called, whom he never hesitated to champion publicly. Yet even when she heard about this the Empress did not withdraw her favour from her protégé, but made up her mind to give him still more protection and to show him still more affection on that account. For from her earliest years she had herself consorted with magicians and sorcerers, as her whole way of life led her in that direction, and to the very end she put her trust in these arts and made them at all times the ground of her confidence.

It is said too that it was not so much by cajolery that she got Justinian under her thumb as by the compelling power of the demons. For Justinian was not a gracious or just person, or so unshakeably virtuous as ever to be proof against such subtle attacks; on the contrary he was unmistakably the slave of his passion for bloodshed and money-making, and powerless to resist deception and flattery. Even in matters which roused him to the greatest enthusiasm he would do an about-turn for no reason at all, perpetually reminding

1. For an account of Mani and his followers see Eusebius, *History of the Church*, pp. 319–20 (Penguin Classics).

one of a weathercock. Consequently not one of his relations, or even of his acquaintances, ever placed any real confidence in him: he was for ever changing his mind about what he proposed to do. Thus, being as we have said an easy target for the sorcerers, he very quickly submitted to Theodora as well: nothing did more than this to increase the affection of the Empress for Peter, as a devotee of these arts. So it was no easy task for the Emperor to remove him from the office he had occupied hitherto; and not long afterwards Theodora insisted on his appointing him First Lord of the Treasury, taking this office away from John, who had been installed in it only a few months before.

John was a Palestinian by birth, a man of very gentle and kindly disposition, who never dreamed of finding means to enrich himself, and had never done an injury to any man alive. Not surprisingly he was regarded with extraordinary affection by the whole people. That was enough to make him thoroughly distasteful to Justinian and his precious spouse; for the moment they unexpectedly found among their ministers a really good man, they lost their heads and were so upset that they made furious efforts to dislodge him at the first opportunity by fair means or foul. So it was that this man John was displaced by Peter, who took over the Imperial Treasury and once more became the man chiefly responsible for great disasters involving everyone. He cut off the bulk of the money which by long-established custom was doled out every year by the Emperor to a large number of citizens as a benefaction, while he himself unscrupulously piled up wealth at the public expense, handing a small percentage of it to the Emperor. Those who had been robbed of their money sat around in great dejection, especially as he took it upon him to issue the gold currency not at its normal value but much depreciated, something that had never happened before.[1]

This concludes our account of the Emperor's dealings with his ministers.

1. For further details see page 166. The currency had of course been depreciated before; the weight of the *aureus* or *solidus* (called by Procopius the 'stater') had dropped in the first three centuries of our era from 1/40 lb. to 1/72 lb., worth respectively £3–15–6 and £2–2–0 at present values. Perhaps Procopius is not looking back so far.

CHAPTER 6

The Ruin of Various Classes of the Community

I WILL now go on to explain how Justinian everywhere ruined the owners of agricultural land. When a little while ago we mentioned the officials dispatched to all the cities, there was no need for us to do more than outline what happened to the countryfolk. The freeholders were the first to be attacked and plundered by these officials; even so the rest of the story shall be told in full.

In the first place, it had been the custom for centuries past for every ruler of the Roman Empire, not once but repeatedly, to remit to all his subjects the balance of their debts to the Exchequer, and that with two objects in view – to make sure that those whose capital was exhausted and who had no means of clearing their debt were not subjected to continual pressure, and to avoid furnishing the tax-collectors with excuses for attempting to inform against men who were liable to the tax, but owed nothing; but the present emperor let thirty-two years go by[1] without doing anything of the kind for his subjects. This meant that those who had no money left had no option but to flee the country and never return. And the informers worried the more prosperous farmers to death by threatening to prosecute them on the ground that for years they had been paying their dues at a lower rate than the payment required from their region. For not only did these unfortunate people shudder at the

1. Procopius reckons Justinian's reign as having begun at Justin's accession in A.D. 518. We have therefore arrived at the year 550.

new level of taxation: they were appalled at the thought of being crushed beneath the unjust burden of retrospective taxation covering so many years. Many were even driven to make a present of their property to the informers or to the Exchequer and let everything go.

In the second place, the Medes and Saracens had ravaged the greater part of Asia, and the Huns, Slavs, and Antae the whole of Europe; they had razed some of the cities to the ground, and compelled others to pay up almost to the last penny; they had carried off the population into slavery with all their possessions, and had emptied every district of its inhabitants by their daily raids. Yet Justinian did not relieve a single man of the tax due, except that he granted captured cities exemption for one year. And yet, if like the Emperor Anastasius he had decided to relieve the captured cities of all the payments due for a period of seven years, I think that even so he would have done less than he should, considering that Cabades had done the minimum damage to the buildings and then gone right away, whereas Chosroes had burned whole cities to the ground and had brought far greater misery than Cabades on those who fell in his path. To these men for whom he made this derisory remission of taxation and to all the others – though they had often been invaded by the army of the Medes, and though the Huns and wild Saracens had continually ravaged the eastern part of the Empire, and the semi-civilized tribes of Europe were doing the same thing all the time and every day to the Romans in that area – this emperor from the very start showed himself a worse enemy than all the foreign invaders combined. For what with requisitions, and the so-called imposts and special levies, the enemy had no

sooner withdrawn than the landowners were brought to
ruin.

The meaning and implication of these names I will now
explain. Those who own farms are compelled to feed the
Roman army on the basis of the tax which each man is
required to pay, the contributions being handed in not to
meet the pressure of the immediate crisis but to suit the
predilection and convenience of the officials, who do not
bother to find out whether the farmers are lucky enough to
have the provisions called for in their possession. This means
that these poor wretches are forced to go elsewhere to find
provisions for the soldiers and fodder for the horses, buying
them all at shockingly inflated prices, and that from a district
which may possibly be a long way off, and then to cart
them back to the place where the army happens to be. On
arrival they must measure them out to the army quarter-
masters, not in the universally accepted manner, but as it
suits these gentlemen. This is the procedure known as
requisitioning, the effect of which has been to bankrupt all
who own farms. For it compels them to pay in annual
taxation not less than ten times the proper sum, since, as
already remarked, besides contributing supplies for the
army they have often had to face the additional task of
transporting grain to Byzantium. For Barsymes, as he was
called, was not the only one who had dared to behave in
this abominable way; before him there was the Cappadocian, and since Barsymes' time all who have followed him
in his high office have been equally guilty. This is roughly
what 'requisitioning' means.

The term 'impost' denotes an unforeseen catastrophe
that falls out of the blue on owners of farms and puts paid

to all their hopes of a livelihood. In other words, it is a tax on lands that have been abandoned or have gone out of production, whose proprietors with all who work on their land have already perished altogether, or else have deserted their ancestral estates and are buried under the troubles that have come upon them as a result of these imposts. And they are shameless enough to impose them on anyone who has not yet gone under completely. Such is the signification of the term 'impost', a word which naturally was on everyone's lips at this particular time.

The question of the 'special levies' we may dispose of in very few words, if we put it this way. Many crushing demands, especially at this time, were showered on the cities, as was inevitable: what prompted them and what form they took I will not attempt to explain at this stage, or my tale would go on for ever. These demands were met by the freeholders in accordance with their individual assessments. But that was not the finish of their troubles: when pestilence swept through the whole known world and notably the Roman Empire, wiping out most of the farming community and of necessity leaving a trail of desolation in its wake, Justinian showed no mercy towards the ruined freeholders. Even then he did not refrain from demanding the annual payment of tax, not only the amount at which he assessed each individual but also the amount for which his deceased neighbours were liable. Beyond this they had to cope with all the other demands which I mentioned a little way back, as resting all the time on the shoulders of those who were unfortunate enough to own farms. And on top of all that, they had to vacate their best and most richly furnished rooms in order to accommodate soldiers and wait on them hand and foot, while they themselves had to live all the time in the most wretched, tumbledown shanties they possessed.

Throughout the reign of Justinian and Theodora all these miseries were constantly afflicting the people, for during this time there was no respite from war or any other major calamity. And as I have referred to the vacating of rooms I must not omit to mention this fact, that owners of houses in Byzantium had to provide accommodation in them for some twenty thousand semi-civilized aliens, and not only could get no satisfaction from their own property but had to put up with a great deal of other unpleasantness into the bargain.

Nor can I possibly leave unrecorded Justinian's treatment of the soldiers, whom he put under the authority of the greatest scoundrels he could find, commanding these officers to rake in as much as they could from this source, on the clear understanding that a penny in the shilling of all they managed to collect would be theirs to keep. He gave them the title of Audit-officers. These devised the following plan, to apply year by year. It is the established custom that army pay is not given to all soldiers alike on the same scale. When the men are still young and have not been long in uniform the rate is lower: when they have seen active service and are now half-way up the list the pay goes up too. Finally, when they have grown old in the service and are nearing the date of their discharge, the pay is much more impressive still, so that they themselves after returning to civilian life may have enough to live on for the rest of their days, and when at last their time is up they may be in a position to leave out of their own property something to console their families.

Time, in fact, is continually raising the soldiers at the foot
of the ladder to the rungs vacated by those who have died
or have been discharged from the forces, adjusting on the
basis of seniority the pay which each man receives from
public funds.

But the 'audit-officers' would not permit the names of
the dead to be removed from the lists, even when large
numbers had died at the same time, chiefly in the constant
wars. And they no longer bothered to add new names to the
lists, even over a long period. The inevitable result has been
that the State never has enough soldiers with the colours, and
the soldiers that remain are kept out by others long since
dead, and so are left with status much lower than their due,
and receive pay at less than the proper rate, while the audit-
officers allot to Justinian all the time his percentage of the
soldiers' money.

Moreover, they impoverished the soldiers with deduc-
tions of many other kinds – a poor reward for the dangers
they faced in war – reproaching some with being *Graeci*[1]
(as if it was quite impossible for any man from Greece to
be worthy of respect); others with being in the armed forces
without orders from the Emperor, though on this point
they could produce a document from the Emperor's hand,
which the audit-officers were impudent enough to impugn
without hesitation; and still others on the ground that they
had been absent for a few days without leave. Later some of
the Palace Guards were sent into all parts of the Empire,
allegedly to scrutinize the lists for the names of any men
quite unfit for military service. From some of these they

1. The Latin word is used contemptuously instead of the Greek
Hellenes.

were brutal enough to remove their belts[1] as a sign that the men were useless or worn out. For the rest of their days these outcasts had to stand in the open forum, begging charitable folk to give them something to eat, to the great distress of all who met them. The rest they compelled to pay heavily for the privilege of not suffering the same fate themselves. Thus it was that the soldiers, robbed right and left, became the most poverty-stricken people in the world and lost all their appetite for active service.

It was this that led to the destruction of Roman power in Italy. When Alexander the audit-officer was sent there, he had the brazen audacity to reproach the soldiers with these very things, and he extracted money from the Italians, declaring that he was punishing them for their policy towards Theuderic and the Goths. And it was not only the rank and file who were reduced to poverty and destitution by the audit-officers: the officers on the staffs of all the senior commanders, a large body of men who had previously been held in high esteem, were crushed beneath the burden of hunger and extreme poverty. For they had no means of providing themselves with their daily fare.

While we are on the subject of the soldiers I will add one thing more to what I have said. The Roman emperors before Justinian's time stationed a huge number of soldiers in all the remote areas of their dominions to guard the frontiers of the Roman Empire, particularly in the eastern region as a means of stopping the incursions of Persians and Saracens. These troops were called *Limitanei*.[2] The Emperor

1. An insult to a soldier's pride.
2. Frontiersmen.

Justinian treated them with such indifference and niggard-liness from the start that their paymasters were four or five years in arrears with their pay, and when peace was declared between the Romans and the Persians these unfortunate men, on the ground that they too would enjoy the blessings of peace, were forced to make a present to the Exchequer of the pay due to them for a stated period. Later he deprived them even of the name of soldiers without giving any reason. From then on the frontiers of the Roman Empire were left ungarrisoned, and the soldiers suddenly found themselves dependent on the generosity of those who were charitable by habit.

Another corps, numbering not less than three thousand five hundred men, had been formed originally to guard the Palace. These troops were known as *Scholarii.*[1] From the start the Treasury has always rewarded them with higher pay than any of the soldiers received. The men whom the earlier emperors enrolled in this *corps d'élite* were Armenians chosen for their merit alone; but from the accession of Zeno there was nothing to prevent the feeblest and most unwarlike specimen of humanity from gaining admission to this exclusive body. As time went on, even slaves by handing over the necessary cash were able to buy the privilege of serving in it. So on Justin's accession this man Justinian admitted a shoal of candidates to this famous corps, thereby making a handsome profit. Then, when he saw that there was not one vacancy left on the roll of the unit, he added the names of two thousand additional recruits, who were known as Supernumeraries. But when he himself mounted the throne, he shook off these supernumeraries in

1. Members of *scholae*, companies raised by Constantine.

double quick time without giving them a penny of the money due to them.

For those who belonged to the main body of the *scholarii* he devised the following scheme. When an army was likely to be sent into Libya or Italy or against the Persians, he used to order these too to pack their baggage ready to join the expedition, though he knew perfectly well that they were quite unfit for active service. They, in terror lest this might really happen, surrendered their pay to him for a stated period. This happened to the *scholarii* again and again. Peter too, all the time that he occupied the position of *Magister*, as it is called, plagued them every day with unspeakable thefts. For though he was mild-mannered and would never dream of wronging anyone, he was the biggest thief alive, full to overflowing with sordid meanness. This man Peter was referred to also in an earlier volume as having engineered the murder of Amalasuntha, Theuderic's daughter.[1]

Besides this body of men there are two others in the Palace much more highly regarded; for the Treasury always allows them a still higher rate of pay in recognition of the fact that they have paid still larger sums for the prestige attached to the service. These are known as *Domestici* and *Protectores*, and never from the start have they come within sight of an enemy: it is merely for the sake of rank and appearance that they apply for admission to the Palace Guards. For a long time now some of these have been stationed in Byzantium and some in Galatia and other places. But these like the others Justinian periodically frightened by the method described already, compelling them to surrender their claim to the pay that was theirs by

1. We had a summary of the story on page 119.

right. This can be explained in a few words. There was a law that once in five years the emperor should bestow on every soldier a fixed sum of gold; and every fifth year they sent to all parts of the Empire and presented each soldier with £10 in gold. It was quite impossible ever to invent an excuse for evading this duty. Yet from the day that this man took over the running of the State he has never done anything of the kind or shown any intention of doing it, although no fewer than thirty-two years have already gone by,[1] so that this custom has been forgotten by most people.

I will now go on to describe yet another method by which he despoiled his subjects. Those who serve the Emperor and his ministers in Byzantium, either by undertaking guard duty or by handling his correspondence or in any other way, start on the bottom rung of the ladder of promotion, and as time goes on they mount steadily to take the places of those who have deceased or retired, and every man rises in rank till the moment comes when he plants his foot on the topmost rung and arrives at last at the summit of his career. Those who have reached this exalted rank are entitled by long-established custom to a salary on such a scale that their annual income amounts to more than £1,500,000, and besides being amply provided for in their old age they are as a rule in a position to make contributions from this source for the assistance of many others. As a result the business of the State has always achieved a high degree of efficiency. Then came this emperor, who by depriving them of nearly all these emoluments injured not only the officials themselves but everyone else as well. For poverty attacked them first and then went on through the rest who had hitherto enjoyed

1. See note on page 154.

some share of their prosperity. And if anyone were to com-
pute the loss from this source which they have had to bear
for thirty-two years, he would soon arrive at the total sum
of which they were so cruelly deprived. Such then were
the ways in which this autocrat ruined the men in uniformed
service.

Now I shall go on to relate what he did to merchants and
sailors, to mechanics, and stall-holders and through them to
everyone else. There are straits on both sides of Byzantium,
one at the Hellespont between Sestus and Abydus, the other
at the mouth of the Euxine Sea, where the place called
Hieron is situated. Now on the strait at the Hellespont there
had never been an official customs house, but an officer sent
out by the Emperor was stationed at Abydus, keeping an
eye open for any ship carrying arms to Byzantium without
the Emperor's leave, and for anyone setting sail from
Byzantium without papers carrying the signatures of the
appropriate officials; for it is not permissible for anyone to
sail from Byzantium till he has been cleared by the men
employed in the office of the *Magister*. A further duty of the
Emperor's representative was to collect from the owners
of the ships a toll which hurt no one but was a sort of fee
which the holder of the office felt that he should receive as a
reward for his trouble. By contrast the man stationed at the
other strait had always received his salary from the Emperor,
and kept both eyes wide open for the things mentioned
above, and for anything that was being taken to the tribes
settled along the coast of the Euxine in contravention of the
rules governing exports from Roman territory to that of
enemies. But this man was forbidden to accept anything
from those whose voyage took them that way.

Directly Justinian ascended the throne he established official customs houses on both straits and regularly sent out two salaried officers. He arranged for the salary to be paid to them it is true; but he impressed on them that they must use every endeavour to see that he received from their operations as much money as possible. The officers, having no other ambition than to convince him of the strength of their loyalty to him, forced the seamen to hand over the entire cash value of their cargoes, and so discharged their own obligations. That was the course he followed at both straits.

In Byzantium he thought out the following scheme. He created a special post for one of his closest friends, a Syrian name Addaeus: he was to secure a little profit from the ships that put in there, and pass it on to his master. From then on Addaeus never allowed any vessel that put in to the harbour of Byzantium to weigh anchor again, but either mulcted the shipmasters of the value of their own ships or forced them to return to Libya or Italy. Some of them declined either to accept a return cargo or to go seafaring any more: they preferred to burn their boats and wash their hands of the whole business. There were some, however, who were unable to earn their living in any other way: their answer was to treble their charges to the importers and take on cargoes as before. The only course left to the importers was to recoup their own losses at the expense of those who purchased the cargoes. Thus everything possible was being done to kill off the Romans by starvation. So much for that aspect of public affairs.

Another subject which I think I ought to mention is the action which the joint monarchs took with regard to coins of the smaller denominations. The money-changers had always been prepared to give their customers two hundred and ten obols (which they call *folles*) in exchange for one gold stater. Now Their Majesties managed to line their own pockets by ordaining that only one hundred and eighty obols should be given for the stater. By this means they clipped off from every gold coin one sixth[1] of its value, causing loss all round.

When this couple of monarchs had put almost all commodities in the hands of the 'monopolies', all the time relentlessly choking the life out of would-be customers, and only the clothiers' shops were free from their clutches, they contrived a scheme for disposing of these as well. The manufacture of silken garments had for many generations been a staple industry of Beirut and Tyre, two cities of Phoenicia. The merchants who handled these and the skilled and semi-skilled workmen who produced them had lived there from time immemorial, and their wares were carried from there into every land. When Justinian was on the throne, those engaged in this business in Byzantium and the other cities began to charge a higher price for dress materials of this kind, justifying themselves on the ground that they were now having to pay the Persians more for it than in the past, and that it was no longer possible to avoid paying the ten per cent duty on imports.

The Emperor gave everyone to understand that he was highly displeased at this, and published a law debarring anyone from charging more than £16 for twelve ounces

1. Believing Procopius incapable of so elementary an arithmetical mistake, some editors reject the evidence of all the MSS and of Suidas also, and substitute 'seventh'.

of this material. The penalty fixed for anyone who broke this law was to forfeit all his property. The reaction of the public, was to condemn this legislation as impracticable and quite impossible. For how could the importers who had bought the material in bulk at a higher price be expected to sell it to their customers at a lower? The result was that they were no longer prepared to spend their energies in this traffic, and proceeded to dispose of their remaining stocks by selling under the counter, presumably to some of the men about town who enjoyed parading in such finery however much it might deplete their finances, or felt it incumbent on them to do so. But when the Empress as a result of certain whispers became aware of what was going on, she did not stop to investigate the rumours, but immediately stripped the owners of all their stocks, fining them £15,000 in gold into the bargain.

Now by Roman custom this trade is under the control of the Imperial Treasurer. So soon after appointing Peter Barsymes to this office they left him free to engage in any shady transaction he wished. He insisted that everyone else should obey the law to the last detail; but he forced those employed in this business to work for his benefit alone; and without any further concealment, in full view of the people in the forum, he proceeded to sell dyed silk of common quality at a price of not less than £12 for a single ounce, while for the imperial dye, generally known as *holoverum*,[1] he charged more than four times as much. By this means he was able to hand over large sums to the Emperor, and to keep still more for himself without its being noticed. This practice, which

1. A hybrid word like 'automobile' and 'television', meaning 'entirely genuine'.

began with him, has continued ever since; for to this day the Treasurer openly occupies the position of sole importer and retailer in this line of business.

The importers who had hitherto been occupied with this trade in Byzantium and all the other cities, whether operating on the sea or on land, naturally had to endure the hardships resulting from these operations. And in the cities referred to almost the whole population suddenly found themselves beggars. Mechanics and handicraftsmen were inevitably compelled to struggle against starvation, and many in consequence abandoned the community to which they belonged and fled for refuge to the land of Persia. Year after year the whole profit from this trade came into the hands of one man, the Treasurer, who as we have said was good enough to hand a portion of his receipts from this source to the Emperor, but secured the bulk for himself and grew rich at the cost of public misery. We may leave the matter there.

How Justinian managed to destroy all the honours and public ornaments in Byzantium and every city besides will be our next subject.

First he decided to lower the status of the barristers, and speedily deprived them of all the rewards which had hitherto enabled them to live in luxury and elegance when their work in the courts was done, ordering the litigants to take an oath and settle their disputes for themselves. This contemptuous treatment was a cruel blow to the ambitions of the barristers. And after he had deprived the members of the Senate and everybody else who was regarded as prosperous, either in Byzantium or in any other city, of all their property, as we have already seen, the legal profession was left without employment. For people possessed nothing of the least value to go to court about. So in a very little while their once great numbers and dazzling reputation shrank to vanishing point everywhere, and inevitably they were reduced to penury and ended by getting nothing for their labours except insults.

Again, he caused doctors and teachers of gentlemen's sons to go short of the elementary necessities of life. For the free rations which earlier emperors ordered to be issued to members of these professions Justinian took away altogether. Moreover, the whole of the revenues which all the municipalities had raised locally for communal purposes and for entertainments he took over and shamelessly pooled with the revenues of the central government. From then on doctors and teachers counted for nothing: no one was now in a position to plan any public building projects; no lamps were lit in the streets of the cities; and there was nothing else to make life pleasant for the citizens. Theatres, hippodromes, and circuses were almost all shut – the very places where his wife had been born and brought up, and had received her early training. Later on he gave orders that all these places of entertainment should be closed down in Byzantium, to save the Treasury from having to finance the payments hitherto made to the people – so numerous that I cannot estimate their numbers – who depended on them for a living. Both in private and in public there was grief and dejection, as if yet another visitation from heaven had struck them, and all laughter had gone out of life. People discussed no subject whatever, whether they were at home or meeting each other in the forum or passing a few moments in the churches, other than calamities and miseries and a shoal of unexampled misfortunes. Such was the state of affairs in the cities.

The rest of the story deserves to be told. Two Roman consuls were appointed every year, one in Rome, the other in Byzantium. Whoever was honoured with this office was bound to expend for official purposes more than £300,000, a little of this being drawn from his own resources, the bulk from the Emperor. This money was normally handed over to those I have mentioned and to those who were exceptionally short of means, especially to those employed in the theatres, giving regular support to all municipal enterprises. But from the time of Justinian's accession these measures were no longer taken at the proper times: at first a Roman consul was appointed very belatedly, but in the end such an appointment was never seen even in a dream;[1] so that unfortunate mortals were perpetually in the grip of virtual penury, as the Emperor no longer provided his subjects with the customary subventions, but everywhere and in every way stripped them of the little they had.

Now I have said enough, I think, to make clear how this destroyer has swallowed up all the funds of the State, and has stripped all the members of the Senate, both individually and collectively, of their possessions. I think too that I have given an adequate description of the way in which by employing blackmail he succeeded in getting a grip on all others who were believed to be wealthy, thereby stripping them of their property – soldiers, servants of all the ministers, Palace Guards, farmers, landowners and freeholders, professional pleaders; and again, importers, shipowners and merchant seamen, mechanics, artisans, and retail traders, and those

1. Justinian abolished the consulship in A.D. 541.

who make their living from the activities of the theatre;
and yet again, pretty well all the others who are indirectly
affected by the damage done to these.

Next we must speak of beggars and common people, of
the very poor and those suffering from various physical
disabilities, and what he did to all these: his treatment of
the priests will be described in a later volume.[1] First, as
already stated, he took possession of all the shops and created
'monopolies' of the most necessary commodities, forcing
everyone to pay three times the proper price. The other
things that he did seem to me beyond enumeration, and I
would not attempt to list them even in a book of unlimited
length. He penalized without respite or mercy the consumers
of bread – artisans, the very poor, and those suffering from
various physical disabilities – who must buy bread or starve.
For in order to make a private profit of at least £45,000 a
year from this source he arranged for the loaves to be not
only smaller but full of ash; for not even to such a monstrous
display of shameless covetousness as this did His present
Majesty hesitate to resort. And using this as a pretext for
finding means to fill their own pockets, those who admini-
istered these arrangements found it very easy to enrich
themselves quite handsomely, while they brought upon the
poor an artificial shortage that seemed impossible at a time
of such abundance; for the importing of corn from elsewhere was strictly forbidden and everyone was compelled
to buy and eat these loaves.

The city's aqueduct had broken and was carrying only a
fraction of the usual quantity of water into the city. But
Their Majesties took no notice and would not spend a penny

1. No such volume has come down to us.

on it, though there was always a great crowd of people round the fountains with their tongues hanging out,[1] and all the public baths were closed. Yet he lavished money inexcusably on buildings along the shore and other senseless erections, littering all the suburbs with them, as if there was not room for him and his consort in the palaces in which all his predecessors had been happy to spend their whole lives. Thus it was not the desire to save money but the set purpose of destroying his fellow-men that led him to neglect the rebuilding of the aqueduct; for no one who has ever lived at any period of human history has been more ready than Justinian to pile up wealth by immoral means and instantly squander it in still more shocking ways. Only two things, then, in the way of food and drink were left to those who were utterly destitute and wholly without means – bread and water; and the Emperor, as I have already made clear, employed both of these to make life impossible for them, by making the one much more costly, the other quite unobtainable.

It was not only the beggars in Byzantium but also some who lived elsewhere that suffered thus at his hands, as I shall now relate. When Theuderic had overrun Italy, he let the armed guard in the palace at Rome remain where it was, so that some trace of the ancient State might be preserved there, leaving a small daily wage for each man. These men were very numerous; they included the so-called *Silentiarii* and *Domestici* and *Scholarii*, who had nothing left to them but the name of soldiers and this pay (which was hardly enough to keep body and soul together): these two things were to be passed on to their children and descendants. To

1. Possibly 'in a state of indignation'.

the beggars who spent their days in the shadow of the Church of the Apostle Peter, he instructed the Treasury to distribute every year four thousand five hundred bushels of corn. This allowance all these men continued to receive until the arrival in Italy of Alexander the Clipper,[1] who without the slightest hesitation made up his mind at once to strip these unfortunates of all their perquisites. When he heard about this, Justinian, Emperor of the Romans, expressed approval of this action and held Alexander in still higher regard than before.

On this journey Alexander had also victimized the Greeks, as will now appear. The guardpost at Thermopylae had for many years been in the care of the local farmers, who took turns in guarding the wall there whenever an incursion of one foreign tribe or other into the Peloponnese seemed imminent. But when Alexander arrived there on this occasion, he pretended to be rendering a service to the Peloponnesians by declining to leave this guardpost to be manned by farmers. So he stationed regular soldiers there to the number of two thousand and arranged that their pay should not be withdrawn from the Treasury: instead he diverted all the general and entertainment revenues of every city to the Treasury on this pretext: they would be used to provide rations for these soldiers. The result was that nowhere in Greece, not even in Athens itself, was any public building restored; nor could any other improvement be made. Justinian nevertheless lost no time in confirming the Clipper's activities in Greece. So much for events in that country.

1. An audit-officer who saved money by clipping the edges of gold coins.

Now we must turn our attention to the poor of Alexandria. Among the local barristers there was one Hephaestus, who on being made governor of the city put a stop to public rioting by his drastic treatment of the rioters, but brought every imaginable misery on the inhabitants. He started by bringing all the shops in the city under a 'monopoly', forbidding any other merchant to carry on this business, and making himself the one and only retailer. Then he began selling commodities of every kind, fixing their prices, it goes without saying, by the authority of his office, so that the city of Alexandria, where hitherto even the very poorest had found everything cheap enough to buy, was brought down to starvation level. They felt the pinch most of all through his manipulation of the bread supply; for he kept all the purchasing of grain from Egypt entirely in his own hands, allowing nobody else to buy so much as a single bushel: in this way he controlled the supply of bread[1] and the price of a loaf to suit his own convenience. So he soon amassed unheard-of wealth himself, and at the same time satisfied the demands of the Emperor in this matter. The people of Alexandria through fear of Hephaestus endured their sufferings in silence; and the Emperor, out of respect for the money that was all the time replenishing his coffers, could not say too much in praise of the governor.

This man Hephaestus, seeking ways of ingratiating himself still further with the Emperor, devised this additional scheme. When Diocletian had become Roman Emperor, he had arranged for a large quantity of corn to be provided yearly by the Treasury as a gift to the needy in Alexandria. From the start the citizen body shared this out among them-

1. Or 'the quality of the bread' or 'the size of the loaf'.

selves, and they passed on the tradition to their descendants right down to our own time. But from the day he took office Hephaestus robbed those who lacked the barest necessities of as much as three million bushels a year, putting it in government warehouses, and informing the Emperor by letter that up to then these people had been receiving the corn without any justification and without regard for the interests of the State. As a result the Emperor endorsed his action and gave him still more enthusiastic support, while those of the Alexandrians who had no other hope of a livelihood suffered most terribly from the effects of this inhumanity.

CHAPTER 7

Everyone and Everything Sacrificed to the Emperor's Greed

THE misdeeds of Justinian were so many that eternity itself would not suffice for the telling of them. It will be enough for me to pick out from the long list and set down a few examples by which his whole character will be made crystal clear to men yet unborn – what a dissembler he was, and how little he cared for God or priests or laws, or for the people to whom he professed to be so devoted, or again for any decency at all, or the interest of the State, or anything that might be to its advantage. He did not attempt to make his actions seem excusable, nor did anything count with him except this alone – the seizure of all the wealth in the world. I will begin with this.

As archpriest of Alexandria he nominated a man called Paul. It happened that one Rhodo, a Phoenician by birth, was at that time Governor of Alexandria, and the Emperor instructed him to assist Paul in all his undertakings to the limit of his power, so that not a single order issued by him might remain unfulfilled. By this means he thought he would be able to persuade the heretics in Alexandria to adhere to the Council of Chalcedon.[1] There was a native of Palestine, by name Arsenius, who had been useful to the Empress Theodora in the most important matters, and had thereby made himself very powerful and extremely rich,

1. The Council which in 451 had insisted on the union of two natures in Christ.

so that he achieved the rank of senator, though his character was of the basest. This man was a Samaritan, but to avoid losing the power he now held he had decided to call himself a Christian. His father and brother, on the other hand, putting their trust in his power had remained in Scythopolis,[1] clinging to their ancestral religion, and at his suggestion treating all the Christians with shocking cruelty. As a result the citizens revolted against them and put them both to a most miserable death, causing a train of disasters to befall the people of Palestine. At the time he met with no retribution at the hands of either Justinian or Theodora, although he was fully responsible for the whole trouble, but they forbade him to come to the Palace any more; for the stream of protests by the Christians about his behaviour left them no peace.

To get himself into the Emperor's good books Arsenius soon afterwards set off with Paul for Alexandria, to assist him generally and in particular to do all in his power to cooperate with him in bringing the Alexandrians into line.[2] For he affirmed that, during the time when he had been unlucky enough to be debarred from entering the Palace, he made himself thoroughly familiar with all the doctrines held by Christians. This annoyed Theodora; for she kept up a pretence of going against the Emperor in doctrinal matters, as I stated on an earlier page.[3] So when the two men arrived in Alexandria, Paul handed over to Rhodo a deacon named Psoes to be executed, alleging that it was

1. Beth-shan, where the bodies of Saul and Jonathan had once been exposed by the Philistines.
2. i.e. with the Emperor's doctrinal views.
3. Page 91.

Psoes alone who prevented him from fulfilling the Emperor's wishes. Rhodo in obedience to the Emperor's written instructions, which came thick and fast and were most peremptory, decided to torture the man: he was stretched on the rack, and died at once.

When this came to the Emperor's ears, under the strongest pressure from the Empress he at once set everything in motion against Paul, Rhodo, and Arsenius, as if he had entirely forgotten the directives which he had sent to the three of them. He appointed Liberius, a patrician from Rome, Governor of Alexandria, and dispatched several eminent priests to Alexandria to investigate the position. These included the Archdeacon of Rome, Pelagius, representing the Archpriest Vigilius, who had given him full authority to do so. Paul was convicted of the homicide and at once removed from his priesthood. Rhodo fled to Byzantium and was beheaded by the Emperor, who confiscated all his property to the Treasury, although he produced thirteen letters which the Emperor had written to him, adjuring and commanding him to assist Paul in everything that he wished done, and in no circumstances to go against him, so that he should be able to carry out the Emperor's wishes concerning doctrine. Arsenius at a hint from Theodora was impaled by Liberius, and the Emperor decided to confiscate his property, though he had no charge to bring against him except his association with Paul.

Whether he was justified or not in taking these steps it is not for me to say, but the reason why I have described these incidents I shall make clear at once. A little later Paul came to Byzantium and offered the Emperor £105,000 with a request that he might be reinstated in his priesthood, on the ground that he had been illegally deprived of it. Justinian received the money graciously and treated the man with great respect, agreeing to make him archpriest of Alex- andria immediately, although another now occupied that position – as if he did not know that he himself had executed those who had lived with Paul and had dared to assist him, and had deprived them of their possessions. So the Augustus[1] flung himself into the scheme with enthusiasm and exerted himself to the utmost, and Paul was confidently expected to get back his priesthood by hook or by crook. But Vigilius, who was in Byzantium at the time, flatly refused to yield to the Emperor if he should issue such instructions: he declared that it was impossible for him to reverse his own decision – meaning the verdict given by Pelagius. Could anything prove more conclusively that nothing ever mattered to the Emperor but laying his hands on other people's property?

Now we come to another incident. Faustinus was a native of Palestine. He was a Samaritan by descent, but had become a nominal Christian under pressure from the law. This Faustinus had attained the rank of senator and had become governor of the region; but he was soon removed from office and proceeded to Byzantium, where some of the priests denounced him, alleging that he had observed the customs of the Samaritans and had treated atrociously the Christians resident in Palestine. Justinian appeared to be very angry and highly indignant at the thought that while he was master of the Roman Empire the name of Christ should be insulted by anyone. So the Senate inquired into

---

1. *Augustus* (in Greek *Sebastos*) and *Caesar* were titles assumed by every Roman emperor.

the matter, and under heavy pressure from the Emperor sentenced Faustinus to be deported. But as soon as the Emperor had got out of him all the money that he wanted, he rescinded the judgement of the court. Faustinus, restored to his former dignities, was on easy terms with the Emperor, who appointed him Overseer of the Imperial Domains in Palestine and Phoenicia. There he was able to do whatever he liked with no fear now for the consequences. Of the methods, then, by which Justinian chose to defend the claims of the Christians we have not said very much: but even from this brief account it will be easy to draw a conclusion.

Now I will reveal as succinctly as possible how he trampled on the laws without turning a hair when money was in question.

There was one Priscus in the city of Emesa who was remarkably skilled at imitating other people's handwriting, and was a most accomplished artist at this mischievous occupation. It happened that many years earlier the Church of Emesa had been made the heir of one of the eminent citizens. This man was of patrician rank; and his name was Mammianus, and he was a man of very distinguished birth and of immense wealth. During Justinian's reign Priscus investigated all the families of the city we have named, and if he found any persons who were very well off and able to survive the loss of large sums, he would trace their progenitors with great care, and if he could put his hand on any old letters of theirs, he forged documents purporting to have been written by them. In these they promised to pay Mammianus large sums which they were supposed to have received from him in return for a mortgage. The amount of money acknowledged in these forged documents totalled not less than £1,500,000. At the time when Mammianus was still alive there was a man with a great reputation for honesty and other virtues, who used to sit in the forum executing all the citizens' documents and countersigning each one himself in his own handwriting. The Romans call such a man a *tabellio*. Priscus made a devilishly clever imitation of this man's writing, and handed the documents to those who managed the affairs of the Church in Emesa, in return for a promise that a share of the money they expected to collect from that source should be reserved for him.

But the law barred the way; for it laid down a thirty-year limitation for all ordinary claims, the period being extended to forty years in a few cases, particularly those arising from mortgages. So they contrived the following scheme. They came to Byzantium and paid over a great deal of money to this emperor, begging him to cooperate with them in engineering the ruin of their completely innocent fellow-citizens. He gathered up the money, and in the twinkling of an eye he had promulgated a law to the effect that churches should be allowed to prosecute their claims not only during the statutory period but for a whole century. This regulation was to hold good not only in Emesa but throughout the entire Roman Empire.[1] To supervise the new system in Emesa he nominated Longinus, a man of action, and of splendid physique, who later became chief magistrate of Byzantium. Those in charge of church affairs began by lodging a claim for £30,000, on the basis of the documents

1. This law goes back to A.D. 535. The reader must avoid the mistake of thinking that incidents recorded late in the book took place late in Justinian's reign.

mentioned, against one of the citizens. They soon obtained
judgement against the unfortunate man, who was quite
incapable of putting up a defence because so much time
had elapsed, and he knew nothing about what had happened at the period in question. Being equally at the mercy
of the informers, all his fellow-citizens were distressed
beyond measure, especially the leading members of the
community.

When the mischief was already sweeping over the majority of the citizens, divine providence stepped in opportunely
as follows. Priscus, the author of this knavish trick, was
ordered by Longinus to bring him the whole collection of
documents, and when he declined to do so Longinus struck
him as hard as he could. Priscus, unable to stand up to the
blow of such a powerful man, fell flat on his back; and
trembling now and overcome with terror, and suspecting
that Longinus knew all about what had been going on, he
made a clean breast of it. Thus all his knavery was brought to
light and his efforts as an informer came to an end.

This constant and daily interference with the laws of the
Romans was not all that the Emperor did: he also did his
best to abolish the laws reverenced by the Hebrews. Whenever the returning months happened to bring the Passover
Feast before that kept by the Christians, he would not permit
the Jews to celebrate this at the proper time, nor to offer
anything to God at this feast, nor to perform any of their
customary ceremonies. Many of them were brought into
court by government officials and charged with an offence
against the laws of the State, in that they had tasted lamb at
this period. They were then sentenced to pay heavy fines.
Justinian was guilty of innumerable other acts of the same

type; but though I know all about them I shall not include any of them in this narrative, which must shortly be brought to an end. The incidents already recorded will suffice to reveal the man's character only too clearly.

Next I will show what a dissembling hypocrite he was. The Liberius whom I mentioned a few pages back was dismissed from the office which he held and replaced by an Egyptian, John Laxarion. When this became known to Pelagius, who was a very intimate friend of Liberius, he asked the Emperor whether the report concerning Laxarion was correct. Justinian flatly denied it, assuring him that he had done no such thing; and he handed him a letter to Liberius, instructing him to hold on to his office with might and main and in no circumstances to relinquish it: he had no intention of relieving him of it at that stage.

But John had an uncle in Byzantium called Eudaemon, who had attained the rank of consul and had made a great deal of money, becoming for a time controller of the Emperor's private property. When Eudaemon heard the story, he in turn asked the Emperor whether his nephew had been definitely appointed to the office. Justinian, denying all knowledge of the letter he had written to Liberius, wrote a letter to John instructing him to take possession of his office and to brook no interference: he himself had had no second thoughts about the matter. Taking these statements at their face value John ordered Liberius to vacate his official quarters, as he had been relieved of his post. Liberius emphatically refused to accept his orders, he too relying of course on the letter he had received from the Emperor. John then armed his followers and went for Liberius, and Liberius with his own supporters took steps to defend himself. A fight developed and many lost their lives, among them John himself, the new holder of the office.

After urgent representations from Eudaemon Liberius was instantly summoned to Byzantium, where the Senate, after making a thorough investigation of the case, acquitted him, as he had not been the aggressor but had been defending himself when this dreadful thing had happened. The Emperor, however, did not allow the matter to drop until he had secretly forced him to pay a heavy fine. Such was Justinian's notion of truth-telling and straightforwardness.

I think it would be to the point if I mentioned the sequel to this story. Eudaemon died soon after, leaving a host of relations but making no will and giving no instructions whatever. About the same time a man called Euphratas, who had been in charge of the Palace eunuchs, departed this life, leaving a nephew but making no arrangements for the disposal of his estate, which was of exceptional size. Both these estates the Emperor seized for himself, making himself the heir by a stroke of the pen and sparing not one penny piece for any of the lawful heirs. Such was the respect which this emperor showed for the laws of the land and for the kinsfolk of his closest friends! In just the same way he had seized the property of Irenaeus, who had died at a much earlier date, though he had no claim to it whatever.

Another thing that was connected with these incidents and took place at about the same time deserves mention. There was a man called Anatolius who headed the list of senators in Ascalon. His daughter had become the wife of a citizen of Caesarea, by name Mamilian, a man of very distinguished family. The girl was an heiress, as Anatolius had no other child. Now it was laid down by ancient law that whenever a senator of any of the cities departed this life without male issue, one quarter of his estate should be given to the local Senate, while the next of kin of the deceased enjoyed all the remainder. Here too the Emperor showed his own character in its true colours. He happened to have recently published a law which reversed everything. From then on, whenever a senator died leaving no male issue, the next of kin were to share the quarter of the estate while all the rest went to the Treasury and to the account of the local Senate. And yet never before in the history of mankind had Treasury or Emperor been permitted to share the property of a senator.

After this law came into force Anatolius reached the end of his days, and his daughter divided the estate with the Treasury and the local Senate in accordance with the law. Both the Emperor himself and those who kept the register of senators in Ascalon wrote letters to her indemnifying her against any claim on her share, as they had duly and justly received what belonged to them. Later on Mamilian too departed this life, the son-in-law of the late Anatolius, leaving only one child – a daughter – who naturally received the whole of her father's estate. Later, while her mother was still alive, she too passed away. She had been married to a man of position, but had borne him no children male or female. Justinian promptly grabbed the lot, voicing this amazing suggestion, that the daughter of Anatolius was now an old woman, and that for her to grow rich on both her husband's and her father's money would be quite immoral. But in order that the woman might not have to join the ranks of the beggars, he arranged for her to receive £2

a day for the rest of her life, finding room in the document
by which he purloined all this money for a declaration that
he was sacrificing the £2 for charity's sake; 'For it is my
custom,' he said, 'to do what is pious and charitable.'

But on this subject I have said enough. I do not wish to
bore my readers; and in any case no man alive could recount
all that Justinian did on these lines.

I will next make it clear that he has never paid any regard
even to the Blues, to whom he expressed such devotion, if
there was money to be had. In Cilicia there was one Malthanes, son-in-law of that Leon who, as I mentioned earlier,[1]
held the office of *Referendarius*. To this man Justinian gave
the duty of suppressing the acts of violence in Cilicia. Seizing
on this pretext Malthanes did untold damage to most of the
Cilicians, plundering their property and sending some of it
to the autocrat at home, while he unscrupulously enriched
himself with the rest. Most of them bore their miseries in
silence; but those citizens of Tarsus who were Blues, pre-
suming on the liberty allowed them by the Emperor,
showered insults in the open forum on Malthanes, who was
not there to hear them. But he soon knew all about it, and
at the head of a large body of soldiers went straight to Tarsus
in the night. Immediately before dawn he sent his men to
the houses on every side, ordering them to quarter themselves there. Thinking this to be an armed raid, the Blues
put up what defence they could. In the darkness much
damage was done; in particular Damian, a member of the
Senate, was struck by an arrow and killed.

This Damian had been president of the local group of
Blues, and when his death became known in Byzantium

1. See pages 112 and 127.

the Blues were furious and made an uproarious tumult in the city, protesting to the Emperor about the incident and giving him no peace, and excoriating Leon and Malthanes with terrifying threats. His Imperial Majesty pretended to be just as indignant at what had happened. He at once wrote a letter ordering the conduct of Malthanes to be inquired into and punished. But Leon presented him with a handsome quantity of gold; whereupon both his wrath and his fatherly affection for the Blues vanished in a moment. While the matter remained uninvestigated Malthanes came to Byzantium to see the Emperor, who welcomed him in the most friendly manner and treated him as a distinguished visitor. But as he came out from the Emperor's presence the Blues, who had been waiting for him, 'showered blows on him in the Palace, and would have finished him off had they not been restrained by some of their number, who happened to have been secretly bribed by Leon already.

Could anything be imagined more wretched than a state in which an emperor accepted a bribe to leave accusations uninvestigated, and factionists, while the Emperor was in his Palace, did not hesitate or scruple to revolt against one of his officers and make an unjustifiable attack on him? Yet no punishment for these crimes ever came the way of either Malthanes or his assailants. From these facts, if anyone should wish to do so, it would be easy to estimate the character of the Emperor Justinian.

Whether Justinian cared anything for the welfare of the State is made plain enough by the way he treated the Postal Service and the Secret Service. The Roman emperors of earlier days took precautions to ensure that everything

should be reported to them instantly and should be subject
to no delay – such things as damage inflicted by the enemy
on this country or that, trouble in the cities caused by faction-
fights or by some other unexpected disaster, and the actions
of the Emperor's officers and everyone else in every part of
the Roman Empire. Secondly, they were anxious that those
who conveyed the yearly revenues to the capital should
arrive there safely without delay or danger. With these two
objects in view they organized a speedy postal service in all
directions. The method was this. Within the distance that
a man lightly equipped might be expected to cover in a day
they established stations, on some roads eight, on others
fewer, but very rarely less than five. As many as forty horses
stood ready at each station, and grooms corresponding to the
number of horses were installed at every station. Always as
they rode the professional couriers changed their horses –
which were most carefully chosen – at frequent intervals;
and covering, if occasion required, a ten days journey[1] in a
single day, they performed all the services I have just
described. Moreover, freeholders in every region, especially
if their farms happened to be a long way from the coast,
derived great benefits from this system; for every year the
surplus of their crops was bought up by the government
to provide food for both horses and grooms, and the farmers
made a handsome profit. So it was that the Treasury
could rely on receiving the tax due from every citizen,
while those who paid the money got it back again immediately; and into the bargain the State got what it
wanted.

   This had been the state of affairs hitherto. But His present

   1. About 240 miles – a quite feasible distance.

Majesty began by dismantling the postal service from Chalcedon as far as Daciviza, forcing the couriers to go all the way from Byzantium to Helenupolis by sea, much as they objected. So they sail in tiny boats of the kind normally used for crossing the strait, and if a storm happens to fall on them they run into serious danger. For since it is their duty to make the utmost haste, any watching for the right moment or waiting for a hoped-for calm is ruled out. Secondly, on the road leading to Persia he did allow the postal service to continue according to the established plan; but on all other eastward routes as far as Egypt he laid down that there should be only one station for each day's journey, and that furnished not with horses but with a small number of asses. The result has been that events happening in any region are reported with difficulty, too late to be of any use and long after they happened, so that naturally no useful action can be taken, and the owners of the lands see their crops rotting and going to waste, and their profits gone for good.

The case of the Secret Service is as follows. From the first, numbers of agents were maintained by the State. They used to go into enemy countries and contrive an entry into the Palace of the Persians either by disguising themselves as traders or by some other trick. Then after making careful note of everything they came back to Roman territory and were in a position to acquaint the Emperor's ministers with all the secrets of the enemy. The ministers, warned in advance, kept a sharp look-out and were never taken unawares. This system had long been in use among the Medes also. Chosroes in fact, if our information is correct, raised the pay of his spies and benefited by his foresight. For nothing [that was happening among the Romans escaped] him, [whereas Justinian by refusing to spend a penny on them] blotted out [the very] name of spies from the dominions of Rome.[1] This folly was the cause of many mistakes, and Lazica fell to the enemy, the Romans being completely in the dark as to the whereabouts of the Persian king and his army.

But that was not the limit of his folly. For a very long time the State had regularly maintained a great number of camels, which followed the Roman army as it advanced towards an enemy and carried everything the army required. There was no compulsion on the land-workers to act as porters, nor did the soldiers ever go short of necessities. But Justinian did away with nearly all these camels. Consequently when the Roman army of today advances against the enemy its movements are severely restricted.

That is the way things were going with the crucial interests of the State. But it would not be amiss to add a word about one of Justinian's more ridiculous actions. Among the barristers at Caesarea was one Evangelus, a man who had made a considerable mark. The wind of Fortune had blown so favourably for him that he had acquired property of many kinds, including a great deal of land. To this he later added a seaside village called Porphyreon, for which he paid £45,000. When news of this transaction reached the Emperor Justinian, he promptly took possession of the place, giving the unfortunate man only a fraction of the price he had paid for it, and solemnly declaring that it

1. There is a gap in the Greek text which editors have filled in various ways. I have accepted Haury's suggestion, which gives a satisfactory sense.

would break all the rules of propriety for a barrister like Evangelus to be owner of such a town.

But having touched on these matters in this summary way I will say no more about them.

The Arrogance of the Imperial Pair

AMONG the innovations which Justinian and Theodora made in the conduct of official business are the following.

In previous reigns, when the Senate came into the Emperor's presence it was customary to pay homage in this way. A man of patrician rank used to salute him on the right breast: the Emperor responded by kissing him on the head, and then dismissed him. Everyone else bent his right knee to the Emperor and then retired. To the Empress, however, homage was never paid. But when they came into the presence of Justinian and Theodora all of them, including those who held patrician rank, had to fall on the floor flat on their faces, stretch out their hands and feet as far as they could, touch with their lips one foot of each of Their Majesties, and then stand up again. For Theodora too insisted on this tribute being paid to her, and even claimed the privilege of receiving the ambassadors of Persia and other foreign countries and of bestowing gifts of money on them, as if she were mistress of the Roman Empire – a thing unprecedented in the whole course of history.

Again, in the past persons engaged in conversation with the Emperor called him 'Emperor' and his wife 'Empress', and addressed each of their ministers by the title appropriate to the rank he held at the moment; but if anyone were to join in conversation with either of these two and refer to the 'Emperor' or 'Empress' and not call them 'Master' and 'Mistress', or attempted to speak of any of the ministers as anything but 'slaves', he was regarded as ignorant and impertinent; and as if he had committed a shocking offence and had deliberately insulted the last person who should have been so treated, he was sent packing.

Lastly, while in earlier reigns few visited the Palace, and they on rare occasions, from the day that these two ascended the throne officials and people of every sort spent their days in the Palace with hardly a break. The reason was that in the old days the officials were allowed to do what was just and proper in accordance with their individual judgements; this meant that while carrying out their official duties they stayed in their own offices, while the Emperor's subjects, neither seeing nor hearing of any resort to force, naturally troubled him very rarely. These two, however, all the time taking everything into their own hands to the detriment of their subjects, compelled everyone to be in constant attendance exactly like slaves. Almost any day one could see all the law-courts pretty well deserted, and at the Emperor's Court an insolent crowd, elbowing and shoving, and all the time displaying the most abject servility. Those who were supposed to be close friends of Their Majesties stood there right through the whole day and invariably for a considerable part of the night, getting no sleep or food at the normal times, till they were worn out completely: this was all that their supposed good fortune brought them.

When, however, they were released from all their misery, the poor wretches engaged in bitter quarrels as to where the wealth of the Romans had gone to. Some insisted that foreigners had got it all; others declared that the Emperor kept it locked up in a number of small chambers.

One of these days Justinian, if he is a man, will depart this

life: if he is Lord of the Demons, he will lay his life
aside.

Then all who chance to be still living will know the
truth.

Select Bibliography

TEXT

Haury, J., *Procopius, Opera Omnia*, 3 vols., Leipzig, 1905–13; rev. G. Wirth, 4 vols., Leipzig, 1962–64 (Teubner Series). Vol. 3 of the Haury–Wirth edition (1963) contains the *Secret History*.

TRANSLATIONS

Dewing, H. B., *Procopius, Works*, 7 vols., New York and London, 1914–35 (Loeb Classical Library). Based on Haury's Greek text, which is reprinted with English translation on facing page. Vol. 6 (1935) contains the *Secret History*.

Atwater, R., *Procopius, Secret History*, New York, 1927; reprinted with an introduction by A. E. R. Boak, Ann Arbor, Michigan, 1961.

Cameron, Averil, *Procopius, History of the Wars, Secret History and Buildings*, translated, edited and abridged, with an introduction, New York, 1967 (The Great Histories Series). Contains only parts of the *Secret History* but has a general introduction to Procopius.

STUDIES

Rubin, B., *Prokopios von Kaisareia*, Stuttgart, 1954 (in German). Also published as the article on Procopius in Pauly-Wissowa, *Real-Encyclopaedie* 23.1, Stuttgart, 1957, cols. 273–599.

Evans, J. A. S., *Procopius*, New York, 1972 (Twayne World Authors Series). The only book on Procopius in English.

Cameron, Averil, 'The "Scepticism" of Procopius', *Historia* XV, 1966.

Downey, G., 'Paganism and Christianity in Procopius', *Church History* XVIII, 1949.

Gordon, C. D., 'Procopius and Justinian's Financial Policies', *Phoenix* XIII, 1959.

Neither the reign of Justinian nor Procopius himself has yet received a major critical study in English. The following works (of very different kinds) will, however, provide much relevant material about both the author and the period.

Barker, J. W., *Justinian and the Later Roman Empire*, Madison, Wisconsin, 1966.

Brown, P., *The World of Late Antiquity*, London, 1971. A brilliant introduction.

Browning, R., *Justinian and Theodora*, London, 1971. An excellent overview of the reign, with many illustrations.

Bury, J. B., *History of the Later Roman Empire from Arcadius to Irene* (AD 395 to AD 800), 2 vols., London, 1889. Though Bury changed his mind about the *Secret History* between this and the next item, his first edition remains useful, especially on mid- to late-sixteenth-century authors.

Bury, J. B., *History of the Later Roman Empire from the Death of Theodosius I to the Death of Justinian*, 2 vols., London, 1923; reprinted 1958.

Cameron, Averil, *Agathias,* Oxford, 1970.

Diehl, C., *Theodora, Imperatrice de Byzance*, Paris, 1904.

Downey, G., *Constantinople in the Age of Justinian*, University of Oklahoma Press, 1966.

Graves, R., *Count Belisarius*, New York, 1938.

Jones, A. H. M., *The Later Roman Empire, A Social and Economic Survey*, 3 vols., Oxford, 1964.

Krautheimer, R., *Early Christian and Byzantine Architecture*, Pelican History of Art, Harmondsworth, 1951.

Mathew, G., *Byzantine Aesthetics*, London, 1963.

Ure, P. N., *Justianian and his Age*, Harmondsworth, 1951.

Stein, E., *Histoire du Bas-Empire*, 2 vols., Paris–Bruges–Amsterdam, 1949–59.

Dates

PROCOPIUS

GENEALOGICAL TABLE

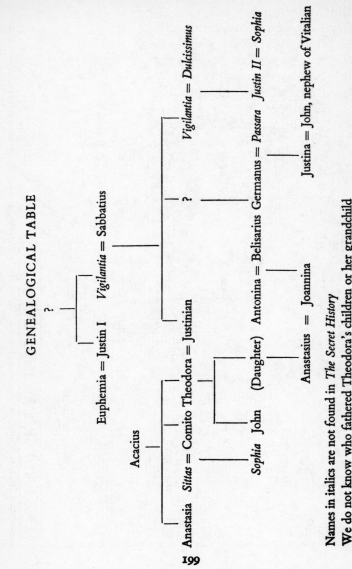

Names in italics are not found in *The Secret History*

We do not know who fathered Theodora's children or her grandchild

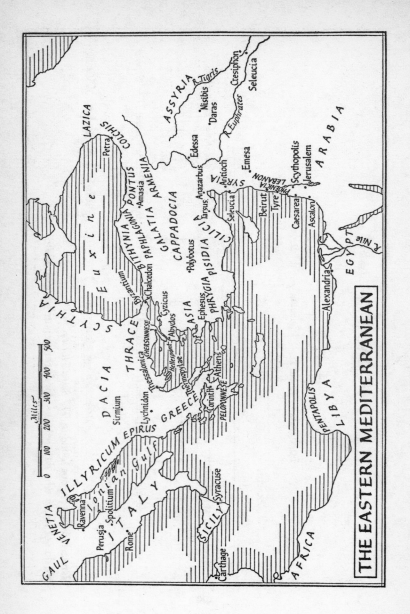

THE EASTERN MEDITERRANEAN

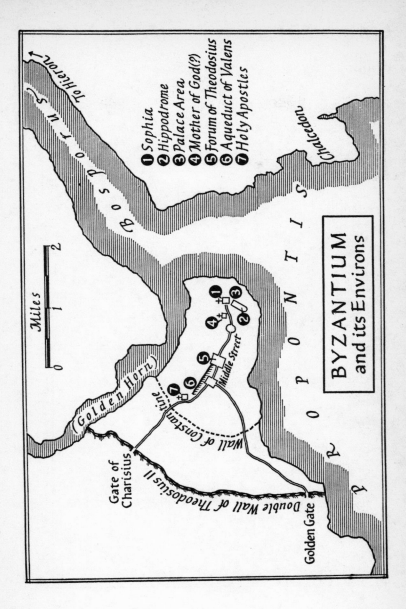

BYZANTIUM
and its Environs

1 Sophia
2 Hippodrome
3 Palace Area
4 Mother of God(?)
5 Forum of Theodosius
6 Aqueduct of Valens
7 Holy Apostles

BOSPORUS

To Hieron

Chalcedon

PROPONTIS

(Golden Horn)

Gate of Charisius

Double Wall of Theodosius II

Golden Gate

Wall of Constantine

Middle Street

Miles
0 1 2

Index of Places

Index of Persons

Acacius, 82
Addaeus, 165
Alemandarus, 96
Alexander, 160, 173
Amalasuntha, 119–20, 162
Amantius, 71
Anastasia, 82
Anastasius, emperor, 68–9, 82, 136–7, 155
Anastasius, Theodora's grandson, 60, 65
Anatolius, 184–5
Andrew, 52
Antae, 95, 132, 155
Anthemius, 100
Antonina, 41–54, 58–66
Areobindus, general, 66
Areobindus, servant, 120–21
Arethas, 49–50
Arians, 96–7, 131
Armenians, 50, 161
Arsenius, 176–8
Asterius, 82

Bacchus, 66
Barsymes, *see* Peter
Bassilius, 100
Bassus, 144
Belisarius, 41–66, 100, 131
Bleschames, 50
Blues, 71–6, 82, 86–7, 92, 104, 123, 186–7

Buzes, 56–7

Cabades, 49, 155
Calligonus, 52, 65
Callinicus, 123–4
Cappadocian, *see* John
Chosroes, 46–51, 55–6, 60, 96, 100, 132–3, 155, 189–90
Christ, 106
Chrysomallo I, 128
Chrysomallo II, 128
Clipper, *see* Alexander
Comito, 82
Constantine, general, 43–4
Constantine, quaestor, 142–3
Consuls, 170
Cyril, 127

Damian, 186
Demosthenes, 100
Diocletian, 174
Diogenes, 122–3
Dionysius, 100
Dityvistus, 68
Domestici, 162, 172
Domitian, 78–9

Eudaemon, 183–4
Eugenius, 44
Euphemia, *see* Lupicina
Euphratas, 184
Evangelus, 190–91